R E T U R N

Translated from the Russian by Ilana Coven

FOREWORD BY HERMAN WOUK

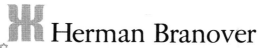 Herman Branover

RETURN

FELDHEIM PUBLISHERS
Jerusalem ✡ New York

First published 1982
ISBN 0-87306-292-2

Phototypeset at the Feldheim Press

Philipp Feldheim Inc.
96 East Broadway
New York, NY 10002

Feldheim Publishers Ltd
POB 6525 / Jerusalem, Israel

Printed in Israel

To the memory
of my parents,
Hertz *and* Devorah

הערץ בן אליעזר

דבורה בת אליהו

ע״ה

ת נ צ ב ה

Foreword

Herman Branover's intensely personal memoir, *Return*, is an impressive Jewish document. It records the physical and spiritual battles of a leading Soviet Jewish scientist to free himself from the bondage of Communist rule, and from the atheism that is the official view in Marxist lands, and the prevalent view in much of free Western society. He won both struggles.

With appalling difficulty, Professor Branover made his way to Israel. As one of the world's authorities in the recondite field of magnetohydrodynamics, he now serves on the faculty of the Ben-Gurion University of the Negev in Beersheva. His pioneer work in the energy field has brought him contracts with the United States government as well.

Parallel to this distinguished life in science, Herman Branover has penetrated deeply into Jewish religious thought and tradition, especially in the field of Chabad Chassidism. He works ceaselessly, in Israel and the United States, as he did in the Soviet Union, to restore to the Jews of our time the love for our heritage that is his own source of strength. As a small part of this unending selfless effort, he arranged for the translation into Russian of my simple work on Judaism, *This Is My God.*

I admire the man and his deeds. I hope that *Return* will inspire many readers to share the powerful Jewish vision of this bold scientist and man of God.

HERMAN WOUK

Washington
Nissan 5740
April 1980

1 This book was originally written as an autobiographical introduction to the philosophical notes I wrote while I was living in Riga in the Soviet Union. These notes served as conversations with myself. Having been educated in the spirit of atheism and dialectic materialism and being thus completely ignorant of Jewish philosophy, I was nevertheless driven by an unquenchable need to find an alternative world outlook to harmonize with my views on nature and humanity as well as to explain the unique place and mission of my long-suffering people in this world.

At first I had absolutely no intention of giving anyone my sketches to read. And I did not dare dream of sending a manuscript outside the Soviet Union. Yet when a possibility of doing so suddenly arose, I jumped at the chance, for I hoped that my thoughts could help others struggling with doubts and longings similar to mine. This decision caused a great deal of unpleasantness for me with the Soviet authorities. Nevertheless, my manuscript reached Eretz Yisrael, the Holy Land, almost ten years before I myself was able to. In Israel, my Russian-language manuscript was translated into Hebrew and published under the title *Mima'amakim* (From the Depths).

The conclusions of my philosophical search led me to see that now, as ever, it is both necessary and inevitable for the Jews to return to living by the eternal, unchanging commandments of the Torah, the *mitzvoth*.

Natural science is my craft, and I was educated from childhood on a basis of rational thought. Naturally, then, I devoted much attention in my notes to the analytic methods and findings of natural science. It would be completely untrue to say that science brought me to belief. However, my search did help me clarify the limits and restrictions of rational thinking, thus helping me overcome my skepticism. One of the attributes of science today, as opposed to a century ago, is that now its limitations, the relativity and non-exactness of its judgments, are plainly evident.

Probably the only conclusions of rational thinking which can be strictly proven are estimations of its own limitations. Therefore, while it is absurd to claim that rational science leads to irrational belief, at the same time there is no reason to hold onto the nineteenth-century assumption that science negates belief.

In the Jewish world, the first carriers of the view that science can negate belief were the *Maskilim* of the "Enlightenment." After them came Jewish socialists of all shades. Today, the majority of the Jewish people no longer feels that belief must be disproved through universal analysis of science or philosophy. Instead, most Jews have simply adopted a rote formula minimizing God, the Torah and the *mitzvoth* as "impossible in today's world."

Here the moral obligation of the Jewish scientist is clear. Anxious about the universal spiritual deterioration of his people, the contemporary Jewish scientist must tirelessly explain the absurdity of the opinion that the modern age is special. He must prove that the penetration of advanced electronics into life and industry has not changed the properties of the soul. Human desires, virtues and vices remain the same.

Someone who understands this will not return automatically to faith and to a Jewish way of life. But at least a major obstacle against doing so will be dissolved. An honest person, in whom the voice of conscience and duty has not been stifled, will not feel that he has to behave differently from his grandfather and great-grandfather. This pretext for pitilessly smashing tradition has laid bare the tender souls of Jewish children to the onslaught of foreign vices. It has doomed our people to forget its mission, to turn instead to assimilation and destruction. To build upon or to restore these ruins, we must first make a clearing.

Belief springs spontaneously in the human spirit. There occurs a moment in everyone's life when the presence of the Creator is felt. When one is overcome by the power of the Creator, then one involuntarily and naturally prays. For belief to become a firm, constant reality, though, the soul must be freed from the chains of prejudice, the coercions of general opinion and of self-deceit. The soul must be fertilized with deep Torah study and observance of *mitzvoth*.

Belief is as natural as breathing and drinking. It does not need an apologia, and by no means do I want what I have written here to be considered as such.

All these ideas were analyzed and discussed in my philosophical sketches written in the Soviet Union during the early 1960's. As already mentioned, these writings of mine were first published in Hebrew in Israel, before I myself was finally allowed to go there in 1972. Several years after my *aliya*, when I was preparing a new edition of *Mima'amakim*, I realized from my experience of living in Israel and visiting Europe and America that most people would interpret my philosophy by assuming that my passion for Torah is merely an intellectual hobby rather than the basis of my life. By that time, I had delivered hundreds of lectures on "Torah in the Age of Technology." And hundreds of times, members of my audience, representing the broad public of Western Jewish intellectuals, had put to me their standard question of belief: "But do you really put on *tefillin* every day and pray? Does your wife prepare kosher food and light Shabbath candles? All this, while living in a modern world?!"

At first such questions infuriated me. People in my audiences were inclined to be favorably disposed to Judaism as long as it remained a beautiful theory alongside many other modern "isms." They couldn't and wouldn't imagine Judaism woven into their lives, making demands upon them.

Yet, fortunately, my listeners have included a few individuals who genuinely wanted to know more about what I meant. They would ask me, "How did you come across this?" For them, a life story is more convincing than theoretical conclusions or abstract proofs. And so I decided to preface my philosophical notes with a description of my life, showing how and why "I came across this." The present book consists of the English translation of this autobiographical introduction.

I do not find it pleasant to publicly discuss my life. Naturally, I tried to shorten descriptions of personal, family and daily life, while concentrating more on my search for Judaism, for faith, for Torah. Nevertheless, to answer "how I came across this," I had to deal with personal concerns, for which I beg the reader's pardon.

2   My childhood was very happy. My earliest and most idyllic memories go back to when I was three years old. We lived in Riga, the capital of Latvia. This small country was independent during the years between the First and Second World Wars. The house in which we lived stood on a quiet little street situated between two old parks. Here silence reigned, but now and then was broken by the thunder of hoofbeats and the rumble of a phaeton. From the porch of our house we often heard the squeaks of a beggarly musician or the shouts of a junkman collecting rags. Our home was on the third floor of a large apartment house which belonged to my mother's father, Ilya Michlin, a well-known pediatrician.

In the mornings my older brother and sister ran off to the Hebrew Gymnasium while I remained with my mother, bustling about the house. After taking me for a walk in the park, she would do her shopping on the way home. Once home, she would light the big wooden stove and start to prepare supper, with me always between her feet, exhausting her with my endless stream of questions.

I was a very sickly and shy child, a real "mama's boy." I

avoided friends and noisy children's games, but adored books, forcing my mother to read aloud to me for hours.

Later, when I was nearly five, I began to read by myself. I read in Russian, as both my parents had finished a Russian Gymnasium and spoke only Russian with us at home. Many of the children's books which I read were published in Moscow and Leningrad. Through them I first became acquainted with Lenin, Stalin and the Red Army, although what lay hidden behind these words I did not yet understand.

Every Thursday my father came home. He was an agronomist and directed an agricultural school for Jewish youth who were preparing to emigrate to Palestine. Set on a farm fifty kilometers east of Riga, the school was organized on the model of a kibbutz. My father stayed there most of the time, coming back to the city only on Thursday and staying until Sunday. He was in love with his profession and had an encyclopedic knowledge of biology and of agricultural techniques. He was constantly fascinated by selection experiments, breeding new types of plants. In addition, he was acquainted with many other branches of the natural sciences. Paleontology and archaeology especially excited him.

When I was only about five or six years old, he began to draw me into his circle of interests. I worshiped his stories about the plant and animal kingdoms. For hours he would read aloud to me from Brem's *Encyclopedia of the Life of Animals.* Together we set up an aquarium, collected beetles and butterflies and cultivated cactuses. My sister, who was four years older than I, also liked animals. Together we bought a pet puppy.

Among my father's many skills was his ability to draw well. During the breaks between our natural science projects, he would try, unsuccessfully though, to teach me to draw. He also made things from cardboard, paper and plywood — marionettes and all kinds of tricks that brought as much happiness to him as to us, his children. He was an exceptionally quiet and shy man: I never heard him raise his voice. He could not bear to hear curse words. Even expressions like "fool" or "the devil" upset him.

True delight would begin for us in the summer when our whole family went out to the farm. It was situated in one of the most picturesque corners of Latvia, not far from the little town of Sigulda. Its hilly landscape and rich virgin forests concealing many small lakes and clear rivers gave this area its nickname, "Lettlandish Switzerland." Its soil is not very fertile and is difficult to cultivate, but the forests abound with every possible kind of berry and mushroom. Bathed by the rain, the air is constantly full of the deep aroma of wild grasses and flowers, all of which the subdued northern sun colors in pastel tones and puts into quiet, dreamlike order.

Here my dear sister and I had several dogs, our own "experimental" furrows in the vegetable garden, and our own corners in the greenhouse and hothouses. Captured from nearby woods and fields, and kept in our house, were hedgehogs, hares, field mice, lizards and often poisonous snakes, kept in bottles capped with gauze. Outside, two domesticated goats would persistently accompany us.

The Hebrew language was constantly heard here. The young people, who called themselves *chalutzim* (pioneers), studied not only agriculture but also the language needed in preparation for their move to Palestine.

I don't remember, though, that Hebrew, which I began to study in school at age seven, or any other Jewish subject, aroused any particular interest or feeling in me then. Of course, I knew that we were Jewish and somehow different from other people. Our school was called the *Zhid* City School, as the Latvian authorities had legitimized in their language the term *zhid* rather than the more respectable *evreye*.

In our school we put on performances on Chanuka and Purim, when we were told about the Chashmona'im, Achashverosh and Queen Esther. Our family always spent the Passover *seder* at the home of my grandfather, Doctor Michlin. Although he did not observe the daily laws of Jewish life, he tried to mark the major annual Jewish holidays. He often went to the synagogue on Saturdays and made an effort to take me with him.

In this way I gained certain, quite disconnected, notions about Jewish history and holidays. I heard that there was a ceremony for Jewish boys at age thirteen called *bar mitzva*. I knew that a long time ago the Jews had come out of Egypt and that they had had strong kings, David and Solomon, and so forth. But I did not have the slightest inkling about most of the Jewish laws. For example, I never heard about *tefillin* (phylacteries) or the holiday of *Shavuoth*, somehow considered secondary in our half-assimilated Jewish circles.

Sometimes I heard the adults talking about someone they called Dubin or, affectionately, Dubinka. From these discussions it emerged that he was very influential, close to the President of the Republic. He helped Jews with various difficult life matters while at the same time teaching them, convincing them of the necessity to observe some special Jewish laws of behavior. In particular, he requested women to visit a special institution called *mikveh*.

I also heard a little about Zionist parties. But this was basically represented to me through the image of my brother, ten years older than I. He was attracted to sports: gymnastics, swimming and bicycle riding. Sometimes he came home with a bruised face, the result of either night skirmishes with Latvians or Germans or of battle between certain groups which bore names little understood by me, such as Betar, Hashomer Hatzair and others.

3 In 1939 our unclouded, measured existence was darkened with apprehension. On the first of September the war began. This was to become the Second World War, and one of the most terrible catastrophes of Jewish history.

Several years earlier, Jewish emigrants from Germany had appeared in our area. Frightened and weary, they had knocked at the doors of Jewish homes and begged for help in burred German speech. They brought a sense of foreboding and warning into the complacent and comfortable atmosphere of the local Jewish community. But they evoked disbelief and anger rather than sympathy. The life of the Jewish middle class was entirely unaffected. Everyone was busy with his own cares of "business" or service. In the evenings people would sit in cafés or gather at friends' houses to play cards.

Even when war broke out in Poland, it was still far away from us psychologically. I remember the day that war was proclaimed. We were at the farm. The *chalutzim* were excited and seemed to be happy. With pitchforks and shovels on their shoulders, they acted out war pantomimes enthusiastically.

Endless debates and discussions concerning the future of the Baltic states began. Everyone tried to foresee who would occupy Latvia — the Russians or the Germans. Property owners like my grandfather, who remembered the German occupation in the First World War, preferred the Germans. Others, particularly those who wanted to check the increasingly pro-German and anti-Semitic Latvian government, favored the Russians.

My father was somehow considered a leftist, although he was probably completely apolitical. Indeed, he was doubtlessly attracted by the stories about the flourishing of the sciences and the extensive opportunities open to Jews in Soviet Russia. He held onto this attraction even though in 1937 two of his brothers in Moscow had been sent to concentration camps on the accusation of "betraying the homeland." Although he knew German fluently, the Russian language and culture were closer to him. As a result he apparently preferred the arrival of the Russians.

On a June night in 1940, Russian troops occupied the Baltic states. Open-hatched tanks came, with soldiers in forage caps and pointed Budenny helmets sitting on the armor. Crowds of people with flowers and red flags met the Red Army. If not the majority, at least many of the welcomers were Jews. Latvians looked upon these Jews with a twofold hatred.

The Latvian president, Ulmanis, addressed his people on the radio, affirming that he would remain at his post and appealing for law and order. This was the last statement of his life.

At first almost nothing changed. Soviet army officers swept into town, bringing along their families. The officers' wives wildly attacked the stores, which were still full of merchandise. Soon, however, queues appeared for products—an utterly strange phenomenon for us, eliciting, therefore, surprise rather than irritation.

A little later more basic changes began to take place. The farm on which my father worked was re-organized from a preparatory *kibbutz* into a regular agricultural school for the local population. My father, however, remained in his former position.

The school where we children studied was also transformed —from a Hebrew Gymnasium to a Russian secondary school, although the pupils and even most of the teachers remained the same. My schoolmates and I welcomed the new slogans and songs.

I became an Octobrist, my sister a Pioneer, and my brother a member of the Komsomol. Excitedly we sang "Vast is the Homeland of Mine," "The Morning Brings a Tender Light to the Walls of the Old Kremlin," "Higher, Higher" and other songs. Eventually, I also became a Pioneer, solemnly taking oath "to honorably and steadfastly struggle for the cause of Lenin and Stalin and for the victory of Communism throughout the world."

There appeared new popular books about the origin of the species and the theory of evolution, as well as science-fiction novels about inter-planetary travel and super-intelligent creatures on the moon and Mars. Darwin's theory so captured my imagination that, with my father's help, I prepared a two-hour report on the subject. I began to pester my teacher to allow me to deliver my lecture to my classmates. I dreamed of initiating a circle of young Darwinists or at least young Michurinists. My teacher vacillated for a long time. After all, I was only nine years old and in the second grade.[1] But I was so persistent that she finally relented.

My disappointment was very deep when after the first quarter of an hour most of my audience were either dozing off, making paper airplanes, or stubbornly concentrating on picking their noses. After half an hour my teacher intervened, and I, pitilessly mangling and crumpling my carefully prepared report, finished my lecture in three-quarters of an hour. There were no questions, alas, outside those asked by my teacher, who was always gentle with me.

In the beginning of 1941 the Soviet regime started to expropriate property. My grandfather was deprived of everything he had accumulated during nearly fifty years of a very intensive medical practice. I remember that as I looked upon his sorrowed countenance, in the depths of my soul I condemned him as a former bourgeois discontented with the Soviet regime. My conflict with my grandfather was further aggravated on Passover when, on the morning following the *seder*, he tried to convince me not to go to school.

Of course I went to school, supplied with a few sweet buns by my tender-hearted grandmother. As I was a Pioneer, it was unthinkable that I would bring *matza* to school with me for breakfast.

That evening my grandfather dragged me to the synagogue, but on the way home I started up a cruel argument, "proving" that religion was nonsense from the position of Darwin's theory of the origin of the species.

---

[1]In the U.S.S.R. children start the first grade at age seven. After ten years of public school, if they wish to continue, they enter a five-year course of university studies similar to a combined B.A. and M.A. program in the U.S.

4　　On June 22 the war rolled in on us. We were at the farm at the time. Within one or two days after the outbreak of war it became evident that the Germans were moving forward so quickly that it was possible that within a week they would reach us. My father deemed it imperative for us to make our way into the depths of Russia, but the lack of a Soviet passport held him back. He was originally from Bessarabia, which had once belonged to Rumania. Thus, at the time of the Soviets' entry into the Baltic states, he was not a Latvian but a Rumanian subject. While Latvian citizens had automatically become Soviet citizens, for a whole year my father had been turned down persistently. Even his former reputation as "leftist inclined" didn't help him.

Now that the war had started, he was convinced that without a Soviet passport we would not be allowed to cross the old Soviet-Latvian border. On the third or fourth day of the war he went to Riga and rushed about to every possible office, but panic, chaos and desertion reigned everywhere. Depressed and distraught, he returned to the farm. In the city he had met with my grandfather, who adamantly stated that he was not going to go anywhere. At that time my older brother was also in Riga and had joined the Komsomol volunteer militia.

One day we picked up a radio broadcast from the Lithuanian city of Shiauliai, already occupied by the Germans. The announcer read, in German, decrees of the new regime concerning Jews. We were only 140 kilometers from Shiauliai. To wait any longer would be madness, but my father, running his finger across the map, still expressed the hope that the Dvina River could hold the Germans back for a while.

A day later it was finally decided to load a wagon with our most essential things and to set off in the direction of Pskov. A horse was even chosen — an old mare named Mayga, which had a wall-eye but was unusually hardy and devoted.

A wide unpaved road crossed the farm about a hundred meters from the main building where we lived. Here for two days around the clock, Soviet troops had been moving uninterruptedly, retreating from west to east. They were traveling by foot, in vehicles, on horses. Occasionally units passed with someone in command keeping something resembling order, but there were hours when ragged and often unarmed soldiers moved along in a kind of disorderly mob. From time to time German planes attacked, and the soldiers ran into the fields, seeking shelter in ditches, behind bushes and ridges.

My parents were getting ready to leave. As daylight was waning, I was standing by the window of the veranda, watching the avalanche of soldiers slowly moving eastward. Suddenly I heard the rumble of approaching planes, just as a column of trucks was passing by. The trucks stopped and the soldiers started to jump down and scatter over the fields. It was already beginning to get dark, and I noticed that the rifle of one of the soldiers jumping off the truck accidentally fired. A commotion began, and within a few minutes I saw a semi-circle of soldiers close in on our house with their rifles raised.

I called to my parents, and my father, seeing what was going on, ordered us to lie on the floor in case the soldiers started shooting and bullets passed through the window into the room. We lay on the floor, listening to the approaching tramp of the soldiers. We knew that the Latvians in the cities were shooting at the retreating Russians from their roofs and windows. So we guessed that they were assuming that the careless shot of one of their own soldiers was an attack from the farm.

Soon their boots were pounding on the porch. The door was flung open and a shout resounded, "Who's there? Don't move!"

Keeping on the floor, we answered, "We're on your side!" We were brought out into the yard. They brought out also all the Latvians, the students of the school. They separated the men and asked, "Who's in charge here?" My father gave his name. Then they took all the men away. As he was leaving, my father cried to my mother, "Take the children and go!" A soldier struck him on the back and shouted, "What's all this talking going on?"

The next day all the Latvians returned. To all our persistent questions about my father they only answered evasively that they had been brought to the next town and then my father was separated from them. My mother stubbornly waited another day or two. She was trying to call somewhere by telephone. Finally, somehow, comprehension dawned, and for the first time in my life I saw my mother weep. I also came to understand that my father had died, but just the same I was not in a condition to feel it. The events of those few days seemed to me to be occurring in a remote, unreal world. They didn't arouse any strong emotions in me. It was as if I was experiencing just another of the high fevers of my frequent childhood illnesses.

That very afternoon — it was the first of July — we found out that the Germans were already in Riga. My mother made up her mind and went to harness the faithful one-eyed mare, Mayga. She gathered several blankets and a coat for each of us, and we set off. I brought a book along with me which I valued more than all else. Called *Traces on Stone,* it discussed paleontological theories and how on their basis the history of evolution of the plant and animal kingdoms of the earth was reconstructed.

For five days and five nights uncomplaining Mayga pulled the cart bearing a defenseless, just-widowed woman, inexperienced with life's difficulties, and her two children — a thirteen-year-old girl and a nine-year-old boy.

The roads were jammed with soldiers and refugees. Everywhere people said that the Germans were within ten to twenty kilometers. We could hear the explosion of close-range fire and frequent airplane attacks. On the fifth day we reached the former Soviet-Latvian border. A border post control was still functioning, but everyone was allowed through with no difficulty.

In several hours we were at Pskov. We brought Mayga to a

courtyard giving her a quarter sack of oats and kissing her farewell.

At the train station, pandemonium and panic reigned. My mother managed to get us a place on one of the open platforms of a long freight train which, according to rumor, would be leaving for the east at nightfall.

We lived on that platform for twenty-three days. The train went slowly, winding around cities and standing for hours at nameless stations. It was hot in the daytime and cold at night. The engine sprinkled us with coal powder, and we ate and drank very rarely, when members of some sort of railway committee brought soup and tea.

The sounds of the war were left far behind as we went deeper into immense Russia. We became acquainted with her through the faces of the ragged, barefoot children who surrounded our train in the out-of-the-way stations. The monotony of all this was emphasized further by the ever-present sign "Boiling Water" under which stood a queue equipped with kettles and buckets.

We passed the Ural mountain range, and our railroad journey ended in Omsk. There we refugees (or officially "evacuees") were assigned to neighborhoods in the Omsk region.

5   We were brought to the village of Tsherlak, 150 kilometers south of Omsk on the shore of the Irtish river.

We were settled into a clay hut, a cob-house, in one room together with an old landlady. All that she could share with us was head and clothing lice. From that time until the end of our four-year stay in Siberia, we constantly were covered with infections from bites and scratches. Every evening before going to bed we spent one to two hours inspecting the seams of our clothing where we would pick the lice out and then burn them in the flame of a smoky lamp.

My mother started to work as a bookkeeper in the office of the *Zagotzerno* warehouses, which supplied us with coupons to purchase products. We hadn't brought any belongings with us and had nothing to sell.

When we became completely famished, my mother exchanged her wedding ring and watch at the market for some loaves of bread and milk. Winter already was setting in, and milk was sold in the form of big frozen discs, shaped like the basin in which it had been frozen.

At that time we moved to a sort of lean-to, two-thirds occupied by an enormous Russian stove for which we had absolutely no firewood.

Forty-below-zero frosts began. Snow drifts reached the height of the rooftops, and inside our room water froze. From time to time my mother procured a few logs, but this was enough only to boil tea, not to add warmth to the room.

I studied at the local school, but most of the time I was ill. It was beyond my strength to withstand the Siberian frosts. Moreover, we were becoming hungrier and hungrier. On the rare days when I did go to school, I was seized by panic at having to face the older pupils. They stopped me on the street and shouted, "Jew-boy! Jew-boy! String him up, ahoy!" Ordering me to say "kukuruza," they laughed at my burred "r." Then they snipped off all the buttons from my torn jacket and, giving me a knee kick in the behind, graciously let me go home.

For a short time my older brother showed up in Tsherlak. The Latvian Komsomol militia had been disbanded. He worked first teaching German at school, then playing violin at the community hall, and finally driving a tractor in a *kolkhoz*. Soon he was called into the regular army, but he had succeeded in earning and leaving us with several sacks of wheat, which saved us from the cold and hungry winter of 1942, the second winter of the war.

6 To save ourselves from hunger, we moved to a *kolkhoz* bearing the high flown name "The Red Banner." But hunger soon caught up with us there, too. People ate carrion, digging up from pits the carcasses of animals dead from a Siberian plague. Children became swollen from hunger.

Summer always brought relief. Vegetables ripened, wild strawberries covered the steppes, and the beneficent Siberian rivers abounded with fish. But winter would bring back cruel hunger.

Finally, my mother decided to move to the Kazakh village. Alongside the "Soviet" law there existed the unofficial "Kazakh" law based on "one hand washing the other." As a result, the inhabitants succeeded in keeping a part of their wheat and lambs for their own use.

But on the other hand here was another scourge. Countless diseases spread from the filth. Children's hands were mottled with itch, their eyes were dimmed and blinded by trachoma, and their heads were deprived of hair and sprinkled with white, flourlike tetter. All this frightened and shocked me.

There was no Russian school, but my mother obtained textbooks for me. I learned them almost by heart and solved all the problems. Thus I finished the fifth and sixth grades. In the remaining time, I did all kinds of daily writing—about the weather, about food, and so forth. I also began to write stories. I remember that the first story which I wrote was about people making a flight to Mars and returning to Earth. I held my heroes in great reverence.

I reached my thirteenth birthday at the Kazakh village. There is no need to point out that I did not celebrate a *bar mitzva*. But perhaps it is proper to point out that then I did not even recollect that, for a Jewish boy, turning thirteen had a particular significance.

The oppression of hunger was ended by our move to the village. But cold, lice, and malaria tormented us as before. Malaria tortured all three of us, but for each one it had a different form — the one-day, the two-day and the tropical form. I was cured by yellow tablets of quinine which my mother provided, through some miracle.

My mother had been transformed from a delicate bourgeois daughter into a fearless Siberian woman. Even the local inhabitants were amazed at her courage when, in the performance of her bookkeeping duties, she would set off to the district center thirty kilometers away by sleigh, completely alone in minus-forty-degree frost. It was not rare for her to return home deep into the night. More than once she told us how wolves had pursued her. As I lay on a wooden cot in an unheated room, shivering from the cold and from malarial chills, I would imagine across the boundless steppes white from snow, covered by a black endless sky, a sleigh moving forward. The horse gallops. In the sleigh sits a small woman wrapped in a giant sheepskin coat. Behind the sleigh, now gaining on it, now falling back, a pack of wolves is moving. Their howls freeze the heart, their green eyes flash. . . . .

7   In November of 1944 a letter came from my brother at the front, in which he reported that he had been in Riga. He wrote that he had not found any of the relatives and that, although it was not yet entirely clear, it should be assumed that they had been killed by the Germans.

Until that time we had known almost nothing about the annihilation of a large part of European Jewry. We received newspapers fairly regularly, although usually many days late. But it was impossible to get an adequate presentation from the Soviet press of the essence and scale of the Jewish tragedy. Much time had yet to pass until the words "ghetto," "aktion," "gas chamber" and "mobile gas chamber" were known to us and their terrible meaning became clear.

On May 9, 1945, the war ended. Two months later we returned to Riga. Externally nothing had changed there. It was summer, and the city parks were just as dense, green and carefully tended as four years before. In the old city there were, in truth, some ruins, but otherwise the external appearance of the city betrayed nothing of the past war. Carriages and taxis traveled about, trams clanged, and in the famous Riga bazaar, Latvian women in starched white aprons sold aromatic garden strawberries and thick yellowish sour cream.

All our close relatives had perished. However, many acquaintances and some of our more distant relatives gradually returned from the depths of Russia.

A large number of Jews who had been living in various parts of Russia, the Ukraine or Belorussia before the war were settling in Riga. Thus the number of Jews in the city started to approach the pre-war level.

On Rosh Hashana and Yom Kippur my mother took me to the synagogue. Of all the big synagogues in Riga only one had been preserved — in the old city, on Paytavas Street. The others had been destroyed, burned (in many cases with Jews having been locked inside them).

In those first Jewish high holy days after the war, the synagogue and the courtyard between it and the street were packed full with people. Many wore military uniforms, some with shoulder straps of high officer rank. Most of them came to meet acquaintances, to ask about the fate of near ones. But inside the building nearly everyone was praying, some in ecstasy with tears pouring forth.

I stood close to the cantor, listening to his chanting and the hum of the congregational prayer, which rose in a rich rumble and then subsided. I did not understand a word, but was possessed by a feeling of belonging to something great, penetrated by wisdom unknown and inaccessible to me. I felt that these people surrounding me in a tight ring were united by ties which transcended all I had known previously and that I inexplicably belonged to them.

I was then barely fourteen years old. I resumed my studies at school in the seventh grade. Personal contact with teachers and visits to the library and to bookstores stirred up anew my attraction to the natural sciences.

Soon I joined the Komsomol. I sincerely believed in communism and even more in the "great leader and teacher of all peoples" — Yoseef Vissarionovich Stalin.

This was the time that American atom bombs had just been dropped on Hiroshima and Nagasaki, and nuclear science and technology were rapidly coming into style.

I avidly read all that concerned nuclear physics, and after every newspaper article or popular brochure my confidence was strengthened in my calling — atomic research. I was in a hurry to get to university and therefore, having finished the seventh grade, during the two summer months I conducted an uninterrupted study of all the textbooks for the eighth grade. In the fall I did the eighth-grade curriculum as an extern at evening school and went on like this to the ninth grade.

I spent, then, from six o'clock in the evening until ten or eleven at night at school, but during the day I absolutely didn't know what to do. Preparing my lessons took only one or two hours, and I spent time reading, but my day was still not filled. From having nothing to do, the completely preposterous idea entered my head to enroll at the children's ballet school at the Riga Choreographic Academy. I spent several hours a day training on the crossbars, executing upon command intricate movements of the arms and legs called by strange French names. We also learned how to do classical dances — waltz, polonaise, polka.

Upon completion of half a year, we began to prepare for a students' variety show on the stage of the Riga Theatre of Opera and Ballet. Waiting for my rehearsals to start, I spent long hours in the dark and empty audience section of the auditorium, watching ballet or opera rehearsals sometimes ten or twenty times. I was chosen to participate in the program of the variety show in a chorus performance of Chopin's Polonaise, and with that my ballet career, fortunately, came to an end.

Upon graduating from the ninth grade, I once again studied at the regular day school. The man who taught physics there was considered the best in the city. Whenever he was sober, his classes were really captivating, and, as a result, my partiality toward physics was even further strengthened.

At that time I began to be particularly interested in the theory of relativity. I would sit in the municipal public library for long evenings right up until its closing time, persistently taking notes on all that I succeeded in understanding from the more or less popular books on the subject. The philosophic aspects of Einstein's theory particularly fascinated me. Some of the authors made detailed excursions into a realm of questioning dealing with worlds of four or more dimensions. Reflecting on the possibilities or impossibilities of perceiving or imaging such hypothetical worlds especially excited me.

At last, with my matriculation diploma in hand, I firmly decided to go to Leningrad to enroll in the physical-mechanical faculty of the Polytechnical Institute. Deciding on that step had not been very easy because I was sixteen-and-a-half years old and still a mama's boy, completely untrained and inexperienced in independent living. In everything, outside of my scientific passions, my mother took care of me and directed me. I shared all my thoughts with her and followed all her instructions. So well did she know and understand me that often in a conversation I did not manage to utter more than the first word and she was already able to complete my whole sentence. She taught me honesty and straightforwardness; she tried to instill in me diligence and a sense of compassion and readiness to help others. She herself had always been modest and shy, and therefore was not able to teach me the boldness so necessary for the independent life into which I was entering.

8 Thus I departed for Leningrad, full of optimistic expectations and dreams of scientific pursuits and other lofty subjects. I was then, as has been said already, sixteen-and-a-half years old.

At the platform of the Warsaw railroad station I was met by Uncle Naum, a cousin of my mother. He was a widower whose wife had died of hunger during the seige of Leningrad. They had never had any children.

He received me like a son. He had a room in a large communal apartment on the Petrogradsky side. This once-splendid dwelling was now occupied by five families, with shared kitchen and hallways, presenting a classic example of a communal apartment. There I saw for the first time a kitchen with five tables and five primus burners. Even more amusing: in the bathrooms there were five separate lights. Next to the light switches on the wall hung a homemade placard on which was written: "Seat! Don't flood it and don't dirty it! Respect yourself and others!"

Leningrad caught me by surprise and won me over. I arrived there in the second half of June when the white nights were already coming to an end. But something of them still remained to excite the soul.

Having come to Leningrad while still a young man, Uncle Naum, like most Leningrad old-timers, was unrestrainedly proud of his city and in love with it. He took me to the great boulevards and squares, to the bridges crossing the silvery brilliance of the Neva River. He took me to Peterhof and to the Tsarkoye Selo

Village and showed me the Hermitage, deriving unspeakable delight from the deep impression which these places made upon me. Even more marked than the clear aesthetic impression of the city was the contact it gave me into with history. For the first time in my life I met things about which I had read in textbooks, in the works of Pushkin and Dostoevsky — places and events which until then I had thought were separated from me by the barriers of irreversible time. The possibility of crossing the bridge over the Winter Ditch, of walking along the casemates of the Petropavlovskaya Fortress, of going right up to the Bronze Horseman, seemed to me, somehow, wondrous.

Leningraders impressed me. Many of them — at least at the time — were distinguished by erudition, by readiness to help one another, and by very touching sentiments toward their city.

However, there wasn't much time for enjoying interesting sights. My entrance examinations were approaching, and I had to prepare for them.

The exams began. That was in the summer of 1948. Stalin had already delivered his famous toast to the "great Russian people." Mikhoels had been murdered already.[1] The epoch of Jewish newspapers, theaters, and publishing houses was reaching its last days. The era of the Stalin-Zhdanov ideological decrees against "cosmopolitanism" was beginning. Rumors spread that institutions of higher learning were going to be restrictive about accepting Jews, particularly in schools of nuclear physics.

[1]Shlomo Mikhoels was a famous actor and producer of the Jewish theater in Moscow. In 1942 he was chosen to be the president of the Jewish Anti-Fascist Committee, a group of prominent Soviet Jewish intellectual and literary figures who organized to help fight against Hitler. This committee was sent by the Soviet government to Britain and the U.S.A. to raise money for the faltering post-war Russian economy. The $2 million which they collected was given to the Kremlin, but in the persecutions of 1948 the committee was accused of "Zionism" and "sabotage." Mikhoels was killed in an "accident," and all the other leading members of the committee — except Ilya Ehrenburg — were arrested.

I did well in the examinations. True, in the oral examination on Russian literature an unpleasant incident occurred. After I had thoroughly answered all the questions on the examination form, plus several additional ones, the woman examiner threw this question at me: "At what time of day and to whom did Korobochka go after Chichikov visited her?" I, honestly, had read Gogol's *Dead Souls* all the way through more than once, but when and to whom this Korobochka had gone I couldn't recall. "You have shown disrespect to *my* national writer," the examiner angrily accused me, emphasizing the word "my" — and struck me down with a three.

Despite this unpleasantness, my average mark was on the level of the best students taking the examination. Moreover, my three was in literature, and I was applying to the physical-mechanical faculty. Yet when they posted the lists I found myself among those rejected. After the tears in my eyes dried, I started to study the lists in greater detail, and I found nearly fifty obviously Jewish names among those not accepted. I could not find a single such name among those that were accepted. My discovery not only did not console me, but it shocked me even more.

I was ashamed to tell Uncle Naum what had happened, and there was no one else with whom I could share my feelings. The tram ride home from the end of the Viborgsky site of the Polytechnical Institute to Uncle Naum's apartment took close to an hour. But this was not enough time for me to calm down sufficiently to feel able to talk with anybody.

I didn't drink vodka, and therefore all I could do was go to the grocery and buy two pieces of pastry and eat them. Finally, all the same, I had to go home and tell Uncle Naum what had happened. To my great surprise, my news didn't shock him very much. First of all, he just naturally didn't understand what it meant to me to see my dreams of being a physicist wrecked. Secondly, it did not strike him as either impossible, surprising or new that I had been rejected because I was a Jew.

The next morning I went to the Institute to protest and plead my case. I knew that the vice rector of the Institute was Professor Levy. I had seen him once. He had a definitely Jewish appearance and spoke in an unusually thin voice, pronouncing the "r" more gutturally than most Jews. True, I didn't know then that he was called Ivan Ivanovitch and that his father had been baptized.

The secretary didn't let me see Levy, but I firmly resolved to wait for him at the door of his office. Evening had set in already when he appeared, making his way to the exit. I followed him. I was very agitated since I had never spoken face to face with a Professor before. We left the building. There was a strong thunderstorm, pouring rain. We jumped over puddles, and the wind muffled my voice. "Tell me," I pleaded, "tell me just one thing. They didn't accept me because I'm a Jew, right?" He replied something about the equality of all nationalities in the Soviet Union and added that the next day they were going to suggest that those who had not been accepted should enroll in other faculties. Then he disappeared in the wet, lightning-blazed darkness.

I remained standing there drenched, humiliated and miserable, not yet knowing then that, possibly, this moment — when I deeply and painfully understood that I was not like all the others around me because I was a Jew — was the start of the most important and fortunate turning point in my life. I was not able to know then that three thousand years ago the Almighty had said to the Jews: "Here I give you a blessing and a curse, life and death. Choose life." Naturally I did not realize yet at that moment the blessing and therefore far from feeling the happiness of being a Jew, I deeply felt the curse. But this was great progress in comparison to the time when I was certain that I was the same as everybody.

9 In the end they accepted me into the hydro-energetics department. Although this was not at all the answer to my dreams, the studies captivated me. The first lectures on differential calculus made an enormous impression on me. The elegance of the thought, the dynamics of the presentation and the deep philosophy of this subject seemed to me to be a genuine revelation. I would spend a lot of time thinking about what I had heard in these lectures and I bought many books on mathematics, going far beyond the limits of our modest required course. I spent long evening hours reading these books, delighting in the process of comprehending what was written in them and experiencing great happiness when a difficult point finally became clear. These were hours, it seemed to me, filled with profound thought and meaning.

I derived pleasure from the lectures on physics and analytical geometry, less so from chemistry. And having to study mechanical drawing and geodesy was very tortuous. These subjects repelled me by their particular practicality and by reminding me that I was not in the physics department.

Our bachelor's quarters at Uncle Naum's filled with one more tenant. This was Misha Gurevich, the brother of Uncle Naum's late wife. He had just been demobilized from the army in which he had served during all the war and for three more years after it. Well past forty, he had neither a wife nor a place to live, so tender-hearted Uncle Naum gave him shelter.

We all three of us would return home late in the evening, and then Uncle Naum began to prepare our bachelor supper. We sat until long after midnight, drinking tea that was brewed with solemnity by Uncle Naum. There was no end to our conversation, and over and over they returned to two central themes:

the falseness and cruelty of the Soviet regime and the unique fate of our long-suffering Jewish people.

Even though I had already lived under Soviet rule for eight years, all I knew about it was what was written in the newspapers, which knocked themselves out in their servility to Stalin, and what I had been forced to learn in school from *The Short Course on the History of the All-Union Communist Party of the Bolsheviks,* reprinted yearly in millions of copies. Moreover, I of course had read *Virgin Soil Upturned* by Sholokhov,[1] *The Young Guards* by Fadeyev[2] and other books in the same spirit. Here, in Naum's room in Petrogradsky, I first heard about the N.E.P. and the subsequent persecution of the N.E.P. men,[3] about the confiscation of farm land and property, about the blood-curdling methods of the Cheka,[4] starting from the time of Uritsky[5] and Dzershensky[6] up to the apotheosis of 1937[7] when millions were murdered or sent to labor camps without trial or inquest — through the verdict of "troika"[8] courts.

[1]Novel about the establishment of collective farms.

[2]Novel about an underground movement of young people organized to fight fascism.

[3]Abbreviation for the New Economic Policy adopted by Lenin in 1921 to try to save the collapsing economy of the country by allowing private industry and trade. Later, thousands of people who had cooperated with this plan (the "NEPmen") were arrested and brutally persecuted.

[4]Russian abbreviation for "Extraordinary Commission," the first name given to the secret police system which was founded in November 1917 to wipe out counter-revolution, speculation and sabotage in the new Communist regime through refined methods of murder, detention in concentration camps and confiscation of property.

[5]First chairman of Petrograd Cheka.

[6]First head of the Soviet national Cheka.

[7]The climax of mass arrests, fixed trials, murders and concentration camp convictions through which Stalin "purged" the Communist party and secured his despotism.

[8]Three-man commissions appointed by the Cheka which condemned political prisoners and used absolutely no ordinary tribunal processes.

But if all this was disturbing and depressing, the stories of my mentors about the past and present of the Jewish people excited and aroused my soul. I found out about the heroic period of the Judean and Israelite kingdoms, and about the tragedies of the Babylonian captivity and the Roman slavery. From these ancient times we proceeded to the life of the Jews in the Pale of Settlement, to the pogroms, to the Beilis affair,[9] to the hardships and persecutions during the civil war between the Reds and the Whites, to the rise of Jews within the arts and sciences with the Soviet regime, and, finally, to the new period of persecution just starting. Our conversation hardly touched upon the State of Israel, proclaimed half a year earlier. It must be said that for me this event had occurred almost unnoticed. I, naturally, had read about it and about the subsequent war, in which the Soviet Union at first had taken the side of the Jews and had even denounced the "Arab nationalists" in the press. However, the proclamation of the Jewish state had not seriously excited either myself or anybody around me. In any case, I had not felt that this event had direct bearing on me. Now, in the course of our nocturnal discussions, it gained greater importance and immediacy in my imagination.

Both of my interlocutors were unusually proud of the wisdom of the Jewish people. Yet the Prophets and the compilers of the Talmud, although mentioned in part, did not serve as much as a measure of this wisdom for them as did the innumerable names of Jewish scientists, writers and musicians. They received great pleasure in compiling long lists of names in which were found Einstein and Disraeli, Spinoza and Karl Marx, Tarle the Soviet academician and historian, Joffe the physicist, Ilf the

[9]Public trial held in Kiev in 1913 against a Jew, Mendel Beilis, accused of having murdered a Christian boy in order to use his blood for Jewish ritual purposes. Although Beilis was acquitted, the trial gave vent to the virulent anti-Semitism of Czarist Russia.

writer, Dubnov the historian, Feuchtwanger the writer and many, many more. Paradoxically, neither Maimonides nor Yehuda Halevi, nor the Baal Shem Tov, nor Rabbi Yochanan ben Zakkai, nor even Moshe Rabbeinu found themselves on this list. However, at the time I did not notice this tragi-comic paradox.

Naum and Misha often had long arguments analyzing this or that dubious case, for example whether the composer Bizet was Jewish. They composed a separate list of revolutionaries and Communist leaders: Trotsky, Sverdlov, Uritsky, Kautsky, Rosa Luxembourg, Martov, Mekhlis, Volodarsky, Kaganovich, Kamenev, Zinoviyev, etc. Strangely, their clear picture of what Russian Communism was did not exclude the possibility of taking pride in famous Jewish Communists.

In this connection it should be mentioned, moreover, that for them, as for most of other Soviet citizens, the conviction that "the newspapers all lie" did not exclude the belief that there "must be something" in what was written in the newspaper.

Uncle Naum adored newspapers and magazines, and his room was filled with all kinds of collections of complete annual sets, new as well as yellowed by time. He read all kinds of books with great interest, sometimes reading the whole night through. Thanks to his extraordinary memory he was truly encyclopedically informed about the history of Soviet Russia and the Civil, Soviet-Finnish, and Second World Wars; about Soviet literature; about Leningrad, past and present; and, of course, about all questions connected with Soviet Jewry.

10

After a while Uncle Naum obtained for me a book about the Beilis affair (published in the early twenties) and two volumes of a prerevolutionary edition of Dubnov's *General History of the Jews*. By some wonder these books had remained intact at a friend's house, surviving the domestic purges of the dreadful nights of 1937 and 1948.

Dubnov took hold of me, and I read his books several times in succession. This brilliant author's account of the three-thousand-year history of my people stood before me, evoking the events of the present day.

Needless to say, I unqualifiedly accepted all the author's conceptions, not understanding that there is a difference between the traditional Jewish attitude to the holy books and the biblical criticism invented by the Germans and so willingly adopted by the Jewish "enlighteners"—the *Maskilim*.

Following the author, I was convinced that the Five Books of Moses were a literary work, compiled from the creation of many authors living in different epochs, that not King Solomon but an anonymous writer living many hundreds of years later was the author of the Song of Songs, and so forth.

The idea especially pleased me that the numerous strict laws regulating every step of a religious Jew were invented by the authors of the Talmud in order to protect the people, dispersed after the destruction of the ancient Hebrew state, from assimilation and annihilation. This idea so captivated me that I wrote a poem, the last verse of which I remember to this day:

Praise, praise to the Talmud's creation,
Able to save us by its sages,
And to the mortal sons of an eternal nation,
Showing the way through the darkness of ages.

My sensitivity to everything Jewish sharpened remarkably. At that time there appeared in *Pravda* an article by Ilya Ehrenburg, which unfortunately later became famous. Taking a full page, he argued that there is no Jewish problem in the Soviet Union and that, moreover, according to Leninist-Stalinist doctrine the Jewish people simply doesn't exist. "All the unity of the Jews of other countries," it said, "is based on their oppression. This is the same as if the whole world started to persecute redheaded or snub-nosed people . . ." Hence it follows that as no one oppresses the Jews in the Soviet Union, then that which unites them with Jews in other countries no longer exists.

In no way could I reconcile myself with the role of a member of a community of redheads or snub-nosed persons. With even more persistence now I tried to understand what my people was and what was its nonpareil uniqueness which I was sensing more and more.

At that time anti-Semitism from "above" was increasing, agitating and strengthening anti-Semitism from "below." It became more and more difficult for Jews to enter certain departments of institutes of higher learning and to advance in work. There were cases of arrests and expulsions. There were many rumors about lists of Jews wanting to go to Israel which were given to Stalin by Golda Meyerson, the first ambassador of the State of Israel to the U.S.S.R. Many terrible stories were told about the fate of the people mentioned on the lists.

About that time I initiated a desperate attempt to renew and to further my knowledge of Hebrew. I was limited to what I remembered from the first grade of the Hebrew Gymnasium nine years before, and this was hardly more than an uncertain knowledge of the alphabet.

I went to the Saltikov-Schedrin Library and, wasting much time roaming through the catalogues, finally found a few textbooks on ancient Hebrew for Russian readers, published in Vilna before the revolution. I spent many hours filling notebook pages with grammatical exercises while also compiling my own Hebrew-Russian dictionary. After hesitating and suffering doubts, I decided to ask a fellow student to join me in these studies. He agreed, and for the two of us the work became a real joy. Whenever we tired, he would take out a book of lyric poetry and I — of the theory of relativity and quantum mechanics.

Soon, however, our work came to an end. One day, when we came to the library and submitted our book order forms, they asked us to follow one of the library workers.

We walked for a long time along dim corridors, through depositories with the heavy smell of old volumes inducing a solemn harmony. Finally, we came to an anonymous office. The man sitting behind the desk was very courteous and smiled a lot. He wanted to know why and with what purpose we were studying ancient Hebrew. Our answers were incoherent — the more so as we ourselves didn't really understand why we were doing this. I simply felt an internal need for it and this feeling had been transferred gradually to my friend.

All this was very displeasing to our interrogator. His face took on a reproachful expression while sweetly and ingratiatingly he requested us to stop the studies.

When I told Uncle Naum about this, he panicked. For him there was no doubt that the danger was serious and that now we had to be quieter than water and lower than grass.

11 My study of Hebrew was arrested, but my attraction to all things Jewish grew even stronger. Our nocturnal conversations in the communal apartment on the Petrogradsky side became yet more lengthy and ardent.

On Passover there appeared at our home *matza*, which, true, we ate alongside bread. On the eve of Yom Kippur I went to the synagogue and then fasted the whole day, continuing to study at the Institute. In the evening, to break the fast, I bought white bread which I ate while waiting for the tram home from the Institute.

Apart from the technical courses at the Institute everyone was required to study the history of the party. In the *Short Course on the History of the All-Union Communist Party of the Bolsheviks* was a special chapter on dialectical materialism, which was taught in particular detail and depth. We heard lectures and prepared seminars, making abstracts on "Sources," "Questions of Leninism" by Stalin, "Materialism and Empirical Criticism" by Lenin and so on.

In "Materialism and Empirical Criticism," Kant, Mach and other philosophers were mentioned. But we were able to discern them only through fragmentary quotations or through the words of instructors who also, of course, did not possess their own copies of the original works of Kant.

From our Institute library, celebrated for its rich collection of books and journals, Mach, Descartes and Leibnitz had disappeared long ago. I saw with my own eyes how from time to time trucks loaded with shredded and trampled books would pull away from the rear entrance of the library. In these transports the library got rid of, among others, the sixteen volume *Jewish Encyclopedia* which had still been available during my first days of study at the Institute.

Thus, we stubbornly mastered dialectical materialism. After the mathematics and physics books it was very difficult for me to get used to the Leninist style, where abuse and derision of other opinions replaced proofs.

Gnoseology, the theory of knowledge, seemed to me to be the most vulnerable part of Marxist philosophy. I struggled for a long time over its claim that our sensory organs give us the true representation of things. This claim provoked many questions. For example, where is the guarantee that two different people can experience identical feelings when perceiving the very same thing? The argument against the Marxist theory of knowledge which seemed to be the most important and irrefutable was this: if we assume that the totality of our sensations gives us the complete and true representation of an object, then there must be some sort of higher arbiter who knows beyond sensation what this object is. Thus, one of the main tenets of the materialist theory of knowledge contains an admission of a Higher Being.

I began to hunt for philosophy books. Often I couldn't get hold of the work of a certain philosopher, so I had to make do with books about him — or more often books against him.

Whether in depth or superficially, I became acquainted with Plato, Socrates, Heraclitus, Aristotle, Lucretius, Philo of Alexandria, Avicenna, Bacon, Spinoza, Pascal, Descartes, Leibnitz, Fichte, Kant, Hegel, Feuerbach, Mach and others.

The strength of abstraction and refinement of thought of some philosophers fascinated and delighted me, while the inconsistency and naïveté of others annoyed and perturbed me, but it was always stimulating to read. Without even suspecting it at first, I was searching in philosophy not just for an alternative to dialectical materialism, which had become unacceptable to me. I was searching for a system of views, a world outlook which would give me, among other things, a key to understanding the unique essence and unmatched historical fate of the Jews.

I understood, or rather instinctively felt, that the answers to my questions lay in the realm of the irrational. I was realizing more and more that my searches were bringing me to God, Who chose the Jewish people. Toward this end, reading philosophers could give me only indirect help.

These studies helped me to reject dialectical materialism as a system. But materialistic and atheistic views, criteria and measures still controlled me. Their basis lay in my belief, absorbed since childhood, in the theory of evolution and in the omnipotence of twentieth-century science.

Books and lectures on physics, astronomy, biology, science-fiction, and paradoxically Dubnov's *General History of the Jewish People* were the real sources feeding my materialistic outlook. How could I have known then that physics, astronomy, biology and, even more so, Jewish history, were by no means identical with materialism and atheism, but — on the contrary — allowed for a directly opposite interpretation — with great success even!

Thus I already understood the absurdity of materialism. I saw through not only the part dealing with gnoseology, but also through its fundamental premise, its desire to turn spirit into a function of material. But I still remained a materialist-atheist, believing that science and modernity itself negate religion.

However, influenced by my strong desire to understand everything Jewish, I gradually became aware of a stronger and stronger need to examine this last thesis. I began to delve into the newest theories in various scientific fields (except for, of course, genetics and cybernetics, which were forbidden by Stalin), searching for clear and direct arguments against religion.

It soon became evident that such arguments don't exist. Already it was becoming clear to me that there is a difference between science, which deals only with the interrelationships of phenomena, and religion, which reveals the essence and purpose of things.

Realizing this difference brought me closer to the conclusion that, as the approaches of religion and science are absolutely different, in principle they cannot contradict one another. I was close then to discovering for myself the difference between "creation from things created" — accessible to science and technology — and *"creatio ex nihilo"* — accessible only to the Most High. Of course, I didn't know these terms then. Only twenty years later was I to learn them from studying Chassidism.

Whatever it was, one of the serious obstacles on the way leading me to Judaism and to Torah was beginning to crumble.

12   Five years of study at the Polytechnical Institute passed. All these years I studied hard and enthusiastically. During the long winter nights I would sit in the Institute library until it closed. Neither the student drinking parties nor the then so popular evening dances interested me. On the eve of Soviet holidays and the official New Year I found myself the only reader in the enormous reading room.

However, as has been mentioned already, I snatched a great deal of time from my regular studies for philosophic and additional scientific pursuits. In addition, all my group at school was very carried away by art. This was a small group of eleven students, seven of whom were Jews. Together we went to lectures on the history of the fine arts and musicology. We spent innumerable days at the Hermitage and did our best never to miss a concert either in the large or small auditorium of the Philharmonic. For several years we attended fascinating weekly lectures on classical music given most successfully by Entelis the musicologist.

It goes without saying that I stayed in the Komsomol. One school year I was even elected to be my group's organizer. I spoke at meetings and repeated trite phrases dug up from the latest newspaper.

I cannot say that the dishonesty of my behavior upset me in particular. Everybody lied. Lying had long ago become a learned habit. The only alternative was to stand up and declare in front of everyone: "I don't want to pretend, I want to leave the Komsomol," and . . . go to Siberia. Alas, I didn't stand up and declare and, I admit, it never even entered my mind to do so.

While in my third school year I began to work in a hydraulics laboratory. Although at first my role was auxiliary, the very fact of participating in scientific research excited me.

I remember how once in the process of work I planned a simple facility, designed it, and gave the draft to the shop. After several days I received my creation prepared. This impressed me as a miracle. It seemed wondrous that my thought, having been transformed first into a conditional drawing of linear design, suddenly became tangible, existing in reality. My work in the laboratory also brought me greatly needed earnings, which together with a scholarship secured for me a modest but fully comfortable existence.

The oral examinations, which were a calamity for many students, were taken by me as a holiday, as a game of chance. I loved to be examined by instructors with whom an exam was turned into a competition, into single combat on the field of the depth of knowledge and quickness of wit.

In the summer we went for engineering practice in building hydrotechnical structures. These constructions were in vogue as Stalin, "the great architect of Communism," had just decreed the commencement of "great constructions of Communism." This included a number of large scale hydroelectric power stations and also the Volga-Don shipping canal.

I spent the entire summer of 1951 on the construction of this canal. I was in the section adjoining the Don River. To this day I see before my eyes the boundless, sun-scorched dusty steppe on which Kazakh convoys with dogs drove colonies of working convicts stretching out to the very horizon. The heat was over 40 degrees centigrade, but the men worked furiously as one day of labor counted as three regular days of their sentence. I became closely acquainted with many of the convicts and heard hundreds of heart-rending stories. I learned something there about hydrotechnics. But undoubtedly the face-to-face collision with this side of life, hitherto unknown to me but so typical of the Stalinist era, was even more important and instructive.

13

I completed my studies at the Institute in 1953. Six months before that, a crisis had broken out for Soviet Jewry: the famous "Doctor's Trial."[1]

I remember well the morning ride on the tram — with its

[1] The January 13, 1953, Tass dispatch in *Pravda* "unmasked" nine Jewish doctors for conspiracy. The charges against them included: "espionage" and "terrorist" work as Zionist, American and British agents; "murder" and "attempted murder by poison" of seven top-ranking military officers; "damage to the health of the Supreme Soviet leaders"; and guilt of having "monstrously trampled on the sacred flag of science." Two of the doctors died under the torture of their "interrogations," but the others were forced to yield the "confessions" planned for them by the secret police. The "Doctors' Trial" set the stage for even more internecine conspiracy and purges within the Kremlin. But all this was abated by the sudden death of Stalin on March 3, 1953.

windows thickly covered with hoarfrost—on the 13th of January in the year 1953. Everything was as usual. The tram crawled through the Viborsky side, squeaking on the curves. I was writing my thesis already and therefore could allow myself to go to the Institute later, after the rush hour had passed. There was even a place for me to sit. I plunged into a book. However, soon I noticed that the heavily wrapped passengers were neither dozing nor reading as usual but were in a state of extreme excitation. Many were conversing heatedly. Through the clangor of the tram the words "Jews" and "Zhids" kept flying at me. I was not able to understand what had happened until I got out at the Institute. Stopping at the first newspaper stand, I found in *Pravda* the notorious communiqué from Tass.

And then it began... Meetings condemning the "doctor-killers" and the "Jewish bourgeois nationalists." Newspaper articles. Newer and newer exposures. If anti-Semitism had prevailed previously with the word "Jew" slyly camouflaged in the expression "rootless cosmopolitan," now suddenly the word was flashing from the newspaper columns.

Quickly, rumors spread about trains being prepared for a mass expulsion of Jews to Siberia. The masses revelled more and more in the permissibility of open anti-Semitism.

Once when I was traveling home late in the evening from the Institute, I was thrown out of the moving tram, accused of trying to stop it with the emergency brake. By a miracle I succeeded in staying on my feet.

Then Stalin died months later, and the "Doctors' Trial" subsided. Undoubtedly the "trial" and its preceding prolonged struggle against "rootless cosmopolitans" promoted a strengthening of my Jewish feelings. At the time of Stalin's death my fondest dream was to reach the promised land of Israel. I remember in that winter of 1952-53 Jaffa oranges arrived at the food store where Uncle Naum worked. He said that the store employees labored deep into the night, destroying the paper coverings in which the oranges had been wrapped. He did not succeed in bringing papers, but he did bring some oranges. It seemed sacrilege to me to eat fruit grown under the sky which was beckoning and calling so. Even though being able to go to Israel some day was not simply unrealizable but even totally naïve to dream about, nevertheless I was returning incessantly in my thoughts to this subject.

During my vacations, spent in Riga, these sentiments were strengthened still more. No matter how strong the official forced standardization in all the provinces of the Soviet Union, in Riga it was still possible to find Jews who were not so brainwashed. Some of them, in a small group of confidants cautiously glancing at a portrait of the "Great Leader," sometimes dared to relate the contents of the last B.B.C. broadcast and sometimes even to talk about Israel. I talked a lot about this subject with my sister's husband, Mark Israeli, a survivor of the ghetto and a German concentration camp. I was very friendly with him.

Once, while in Riga, somehow I got hold of a prayer-book — a *siddur* with Russian translation. Behind the words of the prayers, as I struggled to make out the Hebrew text letter by letter, clarifying its meaning with the help of the Russian translation only when absolutely stuck, a world of cosmic conceptual depth, immense thought, and eternal truth were intimated to me. In this old Vilna edition there were not only translations of the prayers but also some Jewish laws and rules were given. I began to feel discomfort that whereas in theory I was so devoted to the ideas and the spirit of Jewish learning, in practice I hardly fulfilled any of the instructions of this teaching. I began to try to carry something out. My conceptions about the Jewish laws were confused and contradictory, drawn sometimes even from such sources as the stories of Shalom Aleichem. As a result, at the student dining hall I stopped ordering pork schnitzel and requested that butter not be put on the potato puree served with beef goulash. Little did I suspect then that in Jewish law this beef in itself was no less unkosher than the pork which I had turned down.

14 Not long before school finished, we were assigned to places of work. A special commission, headed by a high-ranking official from the Ministry of Higher Education, conducted the assignment. Beforehand, a list had been compiled with the names arranged in decreasing order of the student's scholastic and social achievements. In corresponding order to the list, we had to enter the hall where the commission sat. Supposedly, everyone had the right to choose from the number of places of work left at the moment that his turn came. I was second on the list. Since they had informed us that there were four places open for doctoral studies, I was confident that I would remain as a graduate student in the department of hydraulics. However, when they started calling the students, something strange happened. They didn't call me, not second and not third. I burst into the hall. Stuttering from excitement, I began to explain that probably through a misunderstanding they had forgotten to call me. No one said anything, but two husky fellows seized me by the shoulders and threw me back into the corridor.

They called me seventh and told me that I was being offered work at the all-union institute of the paper industry, Giprobum. I started to protest, and a corpulent man in a military uniform with shoulder straps of a lieutenant-general, looking at me with disdain and condemnation, said: "Offer him Vorkuta, [Siberia,] then he'll agree quickly to Giprobum."

I did not agree to or sign anything. Nevertheless it turned out later that my appointment as an engineer at Giprobum had been confirmed without my consent. The only thing that I could gain at this institute was that Riga was among the many cities in which it had branches.

In the middle of the summer of 1953, when the white nights

were waning, I defended my thesis on "The 200-Thousand Kilowatt Kopchagaysky Hydroelectric Station on the Ili River," received a diploma "with distinction," and went to Riga. Of all the thesis projects on electric power stations proposed to us, I had chosen the one on the Ili because this river flows through a desert. I wished to believe that by working on this project I was acquiring experience which I would someday be able to make use of in my homeland . . .

15 The university was behind me and a diploma "with distinction" was in my pocket, but this did not bring me much satisfaction. Ahead of me lay the sweat of Giprobum — planning the construction of paper factories — whereas my thoughts and dreams were riveted toward two alluring summits. One was called science, creation, discovery; the other — Israel. A way to Israel didn't exist. And the way to science was blocked by many barriers.

I ran to various seminars at the Latvian University, enrolled in correspondence courses at the physics-mathematics department, and took innumerable examinations. At work, putting the sketches aside, I would fill piles of paper with hydrodynamic equations, trying to solve a practical problem which engrossed my attention: the flooding of a hydraulic jump.

Somebody gave me the results of an experiment, the theoretical solution of which was yet to be found. All at once it dawned on me; with a very simple and logical assumption, the solution was obtained. With a palpitating heart I began to substitute the experimental data into the formula obtained. The agreement was perfect. My head was spinning and everything inside me was singing. I felt myself a master of nature; it was obediently subjugated to the offspring of my reason. I was reminded of the words of LaPlace: "When a mathematical solution, proven by experiment, becomes a law of nature, this brings the highest delight available to man."

I wanted terribly to continue the work, to expand it, and to conduct additional experiments. In an abandoned basement hydraulics laboratory at the Latvian University I was allowed, for a certain fee, to conduct experiments. I managed to leave Giprobum and to be appointed an instructor in a college. In order to pay for the experiments, I took on additional work. But with two jobs I could make it to the laboratory only late in the evenings.

16 A little while before this I had become acquainted with Fania, my future wife. On the first days of our acquaintance I flooded her with discourse about Jews, Judaism and Israel. She received it all favorably, with interest — even my philosophic profusions. Thus she passed the principal test, as I saw it, and soon the question of our marriage was decided. True, as I shall narrate later, this marriage was postponed for many years, and the reason was again our longing for Israel.

Fania was studying medicine, but in the evening she would selflessly assist in my experiments on hydrodynamics, sitting in the damp, dank basement sometimes until dawn.

In keeping with an old Leningrad custom, I began to accompany Fania to the museum and to symphony concerts. Her parents, who were as far from Zionism as they were from symphonic music, started to call me "the symphonist."

After a while I summarized all the theoretical and experimental data of my research into a long article, which was published in the scientific journal of the Latvian Academy. It was a joy to hold my first printed work in my hands. I made poor Fania read the entire article. She heroically did this, wishing to please me. From the professional point of view, the article was quite well received. Continuing the experiments and preparing subsequent articles, I proceeded towards writing a dissertation. In this way, it was becoming possible to actually receive a degree without being enrolled in graduate school.

However, before I had time to complete the dissertation, events of an entirely different nature overwhelmed me. 1956 was the year of Israel's Sinai Campaign. It was also the year of the Hungarian revolt against the Soviet regime, which was so brutally suppressed.

In that same year, there convened in Moscow the famous Twentieth Congress of the Communist Party at which Khrushchev spoke for the first time about the "cult of the personality" of Stalin. Whether in connection with these events or independent of them, the end of 1956 was marked by a sharp intensification of interest in Israel among a certain segment of Jewish youth in Riga.

In November or December of 1956 Fania and I were invited for the first time to a gathering at someone's house where the main subject of the evening was Israel. What went on there threw us into a state of great excitement. This was so unlike the usual parties of young people always so repulsive to me, where they drank, danced and joked. Here reigned an idea, an outburst of spirit. We heard tape recordings of Israel radio broadcasts about the Sinai Campaign. We dreamed aloud about going to Israel. We also heard records of Yiddish songs and somebody recited a Shalom Aleichem story from memory.

An argument began. Most of the people present considered "*galuth* melodies" and the Yiddish language to be obsolete and devoid of significance in an age when the history of the Jewish people was being created in the State of Israel and written in Hebrew.

The very possibility of discussing these subjects in a large — albeit carefully chosen — company evoked in us delight and giddiness. We dispersed intoxicated by the whole experience. It is true though that anxiety was mixed with our happiness and that every unexpected knock on the door aroused highly unpleasant feelings. However, as time went on and nobody came to arrest us, we became bolder and more resolute.

Rumors soon cropped up that Gomulka, who had then come into power in Poland, had made an agreement with Khrushchev allowing former Polish citizens who had gotten stuck in the Soviet Union during or after the Second World War to return to Poland. Allegedly, the agreement pertained also to Jews who had once been Polish citizens. Not long afterwards, the agreement was actually published. This was staggering! Walking on the streets side by side with us were people who had the official right to leave Soviet Russia. It was known also that Poland at that time hardly hindered the departure of Jews to Israel. Who could have imagined this a year before?

The only misfortune was that neither Fania nor myself ever had even the most remote connection with Poland.

It didn't take us long to decide what to do. As a first step it was resolved that our wedding would be put off indefinitely. Instead, each of us would register a marriage with a former Polish citizen and go with our fictitious husband and wife to Poland, so that in the end we could re-unite in our homeland.

We were breathtaken by these plans. Everything changed. All our commitments were re-evaluated. In particular, my dissertation, which was already prepared by then, became the first sacrifice of the new initiative. I made this sacrifice without regret. The problem consisted of how to find a suitable bride and groom. Fania had barely reached twenty years of age. Her parents especially feared that we would lose each other in the big world, so they insisted that the bride and groom be sister and brother. This complicated the search for candidates even more.

Despairing of finding someone suitable in Riga, I decided to set forth to Vilna — a city which had belonged to Poland before the war. Having acquired the address of some Vilna Jews with whom I could start my search, and having received a few days' leave from my college, I set out on my way. In the city I was introduced to some Vilniusites, and as they were all connected to a circle of people thinking about Israel, I got the impression that all of Vilna was taken over by departure fever.

Families already preparing for the journey disappointed me. In my opinion, they should have been rejoicing, singing and taking interest only in getting the official papers faster and in finding themselves on the other side of the border. When I imagined someone crossing the despicable armed border unhindered, my heart stopped beating and was filled with an inexpressibly sweet quivering. But these people for the most part were depressed and irritated. From morning to night they were running to stores, buying and packing.

I visited dozens of families, but having gotten nowhere, I returned to Riga. After a week I went again. In the course of two months I visited Vilna no less than ten times. A few times I went together with Fania. The "fiancés" we found were not at all suitable: either they asked for sums of money that I wouldn't be able to scrape together in twenty years, or they declared that they were ready to marry Fania and take her away, but the marriage had to be "for real." I went to Kovno a few times also, but again to no avail.

Unexpectedly, a suitable choice turned up in Riga. One of our Rigan acquaintances was married to a pure-blooded Polish woman. In the time being described here — the early spring of 1957 — her brother Yusek came to visit her. He was not yet thirty years old. As it turned out, he lived in the province of Koshalin in the town of Slupsk, together with his mother and unmarried sister Rufina. I could not have dreamed of a better choice. Yusek had come to Riga not only to see his sister. He dreamed of buying an automobile in Russia and taking it back to Poland. Therefore he was looking for a way of earning money.

We quickly came to an agreement. The plan was simple. Fania and I would immediately stop seeing each other and allow rumors to spread among all our acquaintances and relatives about our quarrel. Fania would start to appear in public with Yusek and go with him to the evening dances at the medical institute where she studied. Afterwards Yusek would return to Poland and send his sister Rufina to Riga, and then I would play at falling in love at first sight. For all this, I would pay Yusek a sum of 22,500 rubles—enough to buy a car plus some other little things.

Everything went as planned. Fania got "married," appeared everywhere with Yusek, was photographed with him a lot, and incessantly shared her raptures with her girlfriends. Eventually, taking with him a brand-new automobile, he left—and letters started coming. The letters were clumsy and primitive, but we were satisfied that the K.G.B. was registering the mere fact of their arrival. As none of Fania's friends knew Polish, these letters could be displayed fearlessly, and they made their impression.

Soon my bride Rufina arrived. I promenaded her through all the boulevards and parks of Riga, dying to run into acquaintances and colleagues. Finally we went to register our marriage. After the registration I moved into the apartment of Rufina's sister. Her relatives were exasperated by my excessive caution and anxiety. They considered the marriage registration quite enough and that acting out a play was unnecessary. I did not yield, and they did not want to give me a bed. So I started to pass the night in their hallway on the floor, fully dressed, stretched out over newspapers.

17 In October 1957, Rufina left. I ran along the platform after the departing train enacting the part of the tormented separated lover. However, I quite sincerely did dream of the time when I would once again see that annoying Polish woman, but on the other side of the border. From that day on I wrote innumerable letters, taking great pains to describe in many lines my unbounded passion. Fania had long since received an invitation from Yusek, but she had not submitted an exit application as it had been decided that I must try to leave first. Finally, an invitation arrived for me from Rufina. By then I had already informed my superiors and fellow teachers at the college that my young wife was pregnant and despite all my reluctance to leave Russia, I was compelled to hasten to Poland so as not to miss the birth.

The director easily gave me the recommendation required for submitting an exit application. I handed in the papers, but somehow I was not totally confident and did not feel any triumph. After a few months they summoned me by telephone, but alas not to the same department of the police where applications are handed in, but to the K.G.B.

At the appointed hour I traveled to the K.G.B. building by trolley-bus. This was to be my first personal acquaintance with this legendary institution, and, I confess, the prospect did not delight me. Before the stop where I had to get off, a woman standing behind me asked if I was getting off. I thought to myself: "With what pleasure I would let you get off here, while I travel as far away as the eye can see — as long as it is away from that dreadful house." However, taking myself in hand, I got off the trolley-bus. The not-so-warming but bright March sun was shining as I walked . . . I wondered when I would see it again.

I was received by an employee whom I recognized without difficulty as an old fellow student from the tenth grade of high school. He had a funny last name — Riyabokon ("spotted horse" in Russian). As a classmate he had been distinguished by tempestuous behavior and insolence and especially had vexed our mathematics teacher.

Another employee quickly joined Riyabokon, and they began to vie with one another in interrogating me. They started roundabout, but gradually they focused entirely on Rufina. They obstinately insisted that the marriage was fictitious. "You wanted to take advantage of her, she wanted to take advantage of you, and she outsmarted you," one of them told me. I categorically denied all the accusations and tried desperately to figure out what they were aiming at. The interrogation went on for many hours—right up until evening, and the next day—the same thing over again. They started to suggest that my so-called "wife" had lost her passport before leaving Riga and in receiving a new one had not indicated on it that she had gotten married in Riga.

I was convinced that they were trying to provoke me, and I continued to deny everything. In the end they made me write out a written explanation and released me. Riyabokon went with me to the corridor. He took me gingerly under the arm and, whispering in my ear, said: "Please, I talk out of friendship towards you. If there is anything not so—admit it. It will be better for you." I again repeated that I knew nothing and demanded that they put me in touch with my wife.

Leaving the K.G.B., I rushed to Rufina's sister. How great was my surprise and despair when it became evident that Rufina actually had lost her passport and, receiving a new one, had not indicated that we were married. "She was afraid that after returning to Poland, Mama would see it registered in her passport," her sister explained.

Thus, our grandiose plot collapsed in a most foolish manner. Nevertheless, psychologically, I simply was not able then to reduce myself to being resigned to the necessity of living out all my days in the Soviet Union, breathing the suffocating air of lies—never to see the Holy Land.

I went out of my way to write love letters to Rufina, and, in accordance, I continued to pretend a total break with Fania. It should be mentioned that ever since the beginning of our "Polish epic" we not only did not meet in public, but we did not even speak together on the telephone. We saw each other once every two weeks in a basement laboratory of the college where I worked. This basement accommodated the student physics laboratory, which I directed. The key to it was held only by me.

In order to agree upon the day and hour of a meeting, we worked out a whole conspiratorial system. I would call Fania from a public telephone on the street. Changing my voice, I delivered a message which had nothing to do with our rendezvous. She would hang up the receiver, and then I would call again. Instead of lifting it up again, she would count the number of rings. Thus I would relay the day, and then the hour of our meeting.

We made our ways separately to the basement-laboratory, under the cover of darkness, and checking that no one was following. In this same basement I buried large polythene wrapped packages of my manuscripts on philosophical and Jewish subjects. The wrapping, incidentally, did not work. Some years later when I extracted the manuscripts, it turned out that the dampness had seeped in and all the letters had run together, making it impossible to read.

Now, after our fiasco, we still continued to see each other only in secret in the basement, as we were afraid to put an end to what at first had seemed to be a hope of being freed from slavery. It went on like this until 1961 when all hope for the Polish alternative was lost and Fania and I acted out a farce in front of our friends of making up. At this time we were married, secretly, according to Jewish law — nearly five years later than we had intended to when the delusive ray of hope had flashed, seemingly opening the way to the Holy Land.

The *chuppa* was held in the town of Dvinsk. We flew there and back all within a few hours. By that time I already knew that the Rogachev Gaon, one of the greatest Jewish minds of our time, had lived there before the war. This was one of our reasons for wanting to have the wedding ceremony there.

Tshernov, the "*shammes*" of the Dvinsk synagogue, and his aide performed the wedding at the *shammes*'s home. Several more Jews were collected from the street and thus we had a *minyan*. We shared with these unknown people the wine and cake we had brought from Riga. They presented us with all their warmth and a most cordial *mazal tov*. We only registered our marriage officially, according to Soviet law, one and a half years later.

18 The wreck of our hopes of emigration brought me to a most difficult spiritual crisis. I was in a state of deepest depression. Everything seemed meaningless, pointless, hopeless. Going on with life in the Soviet Union became simply unthinkable, but to devise a new utopian loophole did not appear possible. There were hours when, as if dreaming, I pictured us in Israel. Nothing could be sweeter than these hours, imagining myself a proud citizen, forgetting about anti-Semitism and above all physically perceiving the Holy Land! But even more bitter was waking up each time to find myself enveloped in a fog of hopelessness, obscuring not only the horizons but also the things closest to me. Desperately wallowing in the fog, I would break out of it only to have it thicken and close in on me again.

It perplexed me how people around me were able to live quiet philistine lives, being happy, laughing. It shocked me how comfortably they adjusted themselves to the all-pervading lies, how with serious mien they were able to read Soviet newspapers and to listen to official radio broadcasts instead of howling like wild animals in insult and disgust. In no way could I understand why the human stomache reacts immediately with indigestion at the smallest quantity of spoiled food, whereas the brain day after day digests tons of thoroughly rotten information with impunity.

A few factors, however, kept me from falling into madness. There were, first of all, the wise and good exhortations of my mother, who, herself a staunch pessimist, always found words of encouragement for me. The countenance of my ever-patient wife

Fania kept me from complete frustration. Furthermore, my philosophical work and my communion with nature saved me.

I was brought closer and closer to Judaism. Questions of gnoseology continued to occupy me. As before, I pondered and read much about the correlations between the rational and the transcendental. But it was becoming increasingly clearer that it was impossible to separate the Jewish people and Judaism from the fundamental and seemingly abstract problems of philosophy. On the contrary, the answer to all questions decisively lay in their profound interconnection.

I had an abysmal lack of knowledge about Judaism. I started to go to the synagogue every Saturday. What I saw and heard there spoke to my heart, although to a great extent it remained incomprehensible. In particular, I did not have the slightest notion about the internal construction of the prayers. I remember that I was so struck by the harmony and order of the service and by how flawlessly the participants knew the responsibilities and times of their performances that I was convinced that the services were preceded by special rehearsals.

At this time I was still riding on public transportation on the Sabbath and turning lights on and off, but nevertheless I tried to devote my free hours on Saturday to studies that seemed to me to be connected with a Jewish theme. I read books on Jewish history or even simply lingered over the letters of the Hebrew alphabet.

I obtained a teach-yourself textbook, and Fania and I began to study Hebrew. I also continued to hunt for prayer books and other Jewish religious books with Russian translation. It was terribly difficult to procure such books, but, even worse, the translations helped very little. I felt that the clumsy language of these translations — much resembling Church Slavonic — revealed only the exterior meaning of these holy books. Their true content, their living soul, seemed to have been hopelessly lost.

Therefore I persistently continued to re-read ten or twelve

times the original ancient Hebrew text. Even though I understood only one word out of ten, and that with difficulty, this clarified more for me than the translation. Here every simple and modest word bore, besides a practical and worldly meaning, a whole world of profound associations and philosophical categories. An aroma of simple wisdom and pure holiness wafted from these words, whereas in the Russian translation the depth was lost, the holiness turned into sanctimoniousness and the purity and uprightness into hypocrisy.

I also became more and more keenly aware of the need for commentaries, for someone wise and perceptive of the depth of Torah to help me and guide me. Not having such a teacher, I would struggle for hours with a single phrase, not perceiving its connection and correlation with the other parts of the teaching.

Contact with the Torah healed my desperation. It raised me above time, space and borders and united me with Israel in a unity over which the K.G.B. had no control.

Ever since childhood, when I would walk with my father through the forests and fields surrounding the farm, I have felt a deep affinity for nature. Nature was for me not an ornament, not a work of art summoning delight, but a living partner in mutual love. And every time that people offended me, this love would be especially strengthened. The dense mossy forests, saturated with moisture and the scent of mushrooms, called me; the meadows motley with flowers and butterflies beckoned. Every year as soon as spring awakened, a deep yearning for nature would drive me away from the lifeless and apathetic stones of the city to the fields and gardens — to where life was being born and triumphing, where the scents of the reviving earth inebriated and melted the soul, releasing exultant hymns to the Creator. Fear of being late for the festival of spring would overcome me. This festival was composed of many events — each one more meaningful than the next. It seemed to me a crime not to witness every one of them.

One morning the trees awake from their slumber amidst the finest lace of sticky baby leaves, and then the bird-cherry tree blossoms in a frenzy, and then the nightingales sing, starting as they ought at night, but, carried away, they continue on the whole day through, and then the lilac blooms, and then the very last to turn green are the pensive, solid oaks, and then . . . Thus spring ends, flying away with the poplar down. The linden trees then burst into blossom and their honeyed aroma penetrates into the cities, flooding the streets, streaming into windows and prevailing over soot and stench.

Now the frenzy in nature yields its place to efficiency — there is so much to be done, you see, in the short northern summer. At sunrise work begins for the birds and the insects, and for those people who still understand that bread grows in the fields and that rain does not just ruin outings but is primarily a blessing for the harvest.

Especially I loved the twilight hours, when the rays of the low sun, setting through the leaves of the emerald-saturated trees, suffused the earth with quietude and subdued light. The last breezes calm down. For some time the lowing of cows returning from pasture and the barking of dogs are heard from a nearby farm and then these voices, too, subside. The earth pulsates, pacified, tired from the day's accomplishments and satisfied with them. In a while, hiding in the cold low places of the dark, tree boughs start to quiver from the awakening night winds, arousing secret nocturnal rustles. And then — silence. And it seems that the world is meditating on the harmony and wisdom of creation.

Autumn evokes the same quiet and peace of the summer twilight hours, extended for many weeks. Weakened from its summer labors, the sun begins to caress and redden the seasoned apples. Long threads of gossamer float in the air until the red-golden carpet of fallen leaves, smelling like strongly brewed tea, is covered by hoarfrost.

The chasteness and purity of nature healed my soul from the poison of cynicism, cruelty and lies which I had to breathe day after day. Moreover, contemplation of the forests and fields led me to thoughts of their Creator and engendered infinite thankfulness and a need to pray to Him.

In the course of a few years, to the extent that I slowly became liberated from my feelings of depression, meaninglessness and hopelessness through the help of these curative influences, so did I progress in the practical observance of Jewish laws. In particular, I finally came to understand the basic rules of *kashruth*. I bought some new plates, spoons and forks. For a long time I abstained entirely from meat. Finally, I found an underground butcher who sold kosher meat from time to time. Keeping kosher, despite all the inconveniences connected to it, brought me great moral satisfaction and the feeling of honestly and voluntarily fulfilling my obligations.

19

Towards the beginning of the sixties there were already several dozen Jews in Riga who displayed their interest in Israel quite openly. They exchanged Israeli books, brochures, calendars. They reproduced copies of old books by Chaim Nachman Bialik and Ze'ev Jabotinsky. They gathered together to hear Israeli records or to learn Hebrew.

Fania and I participated in numerous meetings of that nature, although we were put off by their salon style, by their mixing of the holy and the eternal with exhibitions of awful Philistinism and sometimes with the most banal flirting.

The capture and trial of Eichmann had great influence upon the consciousness of many Jews. Memories of the still-recent tragedy of the Jewish people were stirred up strongly anew. Many Jews who had been listening regularly to Israel radio now did not budge from their receivers while the trial was on. For entire evenings they would listen to the Hebrew, Yiddish, Russian and English broadcasts in succession.

About that time the Rumbula episode came to light. Rumbula is the name of a small railroad station twelve kilometers east of Riga. This name is one of a dreadful series of words like Auschwitz, Treblinka, Babi Yar, Ponari.

In the fall of 1941, in the pine grove opposite the station, the Germans, with the enthusiastic participation of Latvians, exterminated the entire population of the Riga ghetto. Nine abysmal graves hold nearly fifty thousand victims. This place remained absolutely abandoned and was known to very few. Finally, a group of Jews took it upon themselves to bring some order to this fraternal burial ground. With the help of Bella Michelson who miraculously had survived and crawled out of one of these graves almost twenty years before, they searched for the site. Only the extraordinarily thick, high grass growing on them marked out the graves.

At first the group was small in number. It included the lawyer Garber and his wife; the engineer Getz; the young, ardent and unrestrainable Marek Bloom (who appropriately changed his last name after arriving in Israel to "Lapid" — meaning torch); the architect Rachlin and his son (a clever boy, passionately in love with Israel, who was later the victim of Soviet secret-police persecution which led to his tragic death); the artist Kuzkovsky (of blessed memory); Ezra Rusinek, and others.

The true spirit and motivating force of all this was Samuel Tzeitlin, whom everyone called "Bubi." Bubi was connected with Zionism when yet a youth, before the Soviets entered Latvia. Then, fighting the war in the ranks of the Red Army, he was badly wounded. He was arrested while still in hospital and "re-settled" in a Soviet camp for many years. Finally returning to Riga, Bubi remained a bachelor. He worked as a dental technician, which, without burdening him too much, secured him a modest subsistence. He knew absolutely everyone and would sit almost until daybreak visiting with friends and acquaintances, endlessly telling concentration camp stories, debating urgent Jewish topics, and consuming an entire bottle of vodka each night. Reputed to be a great eccentric, he made fun of everyone, himself included. He went about in a torn and threadbare coat and maintained touching relationships with his former camp inmates, including several priests. And he knew how to help dozens of Jewish families and to disseminate hundreds of Jewish books.

Rumbula became his lifework. He endeavoured to obtain the maximum possible support from the Soviet authorities. Wondrously, he convinced them to allow the construction of a memorial, and even óbtained some money for the project.

The work at Rumbula became a weekly activity. Every Sunday a few hundred people would gather together, a great many of whom were young boys and girls born after the war. They paved walk-ways, cleared the site, and leveled the earth. A wonderful atmosphere of solidarity, brotherhood and spiritual uplift reigned. At first it depressed me to be at this terrible place where at each step the earth turned up a bone, a child's shoe. The squeak of the pine trees swayed by the wind seemed to me to be the anguished sighs of those shot down. Even hours after coming home, I was not in a condition to return to ordinary activity. Dragging heavy barrows of gravel, I thought: with what joy would I be working within this circle of brothers if we were not unearthing a cemetery but, for example, building a synagogue. It shocked me how these tender boys who had not yet sprouted beards could be singing songs, here at this grove of death and despair. Sometimes they even nibbled apples carelessly while standing right on a grave. But gradually I got used to this, learning to suppress my feelings. The fact was that these boys working here were progressing rapidly in developing Jewish feelings. This seemed to me to be a compensation for the tragedy of the ghetto. It was a fitting memorial for the annihilated.

Having finished work, the people would congregate. Someone would read or chant the memorial prayer for the dead, another would deliver a short improvised speech, a third read his own poetry. From time to time the speeches grew bolder. The spirit of the Rumbula Sundays prevailed over many Jewish families in Riga and gradually — through relatives and friends — it was spread to Moscow, to Leningrad.

It didn't take much time until Rumbula drew the attention of the authorities. Henceforth we worked under the strict surveillance not only of the secret police but also of the regular police, as well as of cadets from military academies. The after-work meetings were broken up. The homemade monuments on the graves — often an enormous star of David twisted out of barbed wire — were destroyed.

A special storm was raised by the attempt to place a tombstone upon which was written in Yiddish: "Di korbones foon Fascism" (the victims of fascism). The authorities demanded that the inscription be done in Russian and that the slain be called "Soviet Citizens." It was rumored that a special ideological commission of the Central Committee of the Communist Party came from Moscow to Riga just for this.

The finished stone with the Jewish inscription was confiscated. However, Bubi and his friends stole the stone from the engraver's at night, placed it on its prepared site and photographed it. The next day these photographs were seen in foreign newspapers, and the authorities decided to give in.

This stone is still standing.

Twice a year — in autumn at the anniversary of the extermination of the ghetto and in spring at the anniversary of the victory over the Germans — thousands of Jews congregate at the Rumbula cemetery. The authorities break up these meetings, arresting the speakers. Policemen wail into loudspeakers set up all around so that the speakers can't even hear their own voices. They surround the entire grove with tanks and cannons and then tell anyone who tries to approach that war exercises are being conducted.

But in every instance the authorities are the losers. Their opposition inflames the feelings of even the most apathetic Jews.

There is no doubt that Rumbula was one of the most

important factors in the awakening of the "Silent Jews" of Soviet Russia, an awakening which subsequently led many thousands of them toward emigration to Israel.

20 To the extent that I recovered from the shock caused by the failure of our attempt to escape through Poland and began to reconcile myself with the thought that we still had many more years in the Soviet Union, I began to remember my abandoned scientific work. I started to think about a new dissertation to replace the previous one, sacrificed to the hope of leaving the country. A friend told me that in the Physics Institute of the Latvian Academy of Sciences they were beginning to develop a new field of study — magnetohydrodynamics. This term was absolutely new for me, but as it included the word hydrodynamics, it seemed quite likely that I could fit into this field. When I went to the library to clarify what magnetohydrodynamics is, it turned out that this term did not yet appear in even the large encyclopedic dictionaries. Nevertheless, I finally found out that magnetohydrodynamics is the study of the movement of electroconductive fluids in the presence of a magnetic field. Based on the two classical sciences of hydrodynamics and electrodynamics, it can be applied to astro-physics, geo-physics, flow-measuring techniques, to different aspects of metallurgy and finally to the production of electrical power.

I went to the Institute of Physics and told them of my earlier experience in measuring the velocity of flows and turbulent pulsations. To my great surprise, the head of one of the laboratories and director of the Institute literally grabbed me. Certain that because of the blots on my personal record they would not accept me for work at the Academy, I told them that at present I could not leave the technical college, but consented to work at the Physics Institute part-time at half salary. And that is what was agreed.

As a new branch of science, magnetohydrodynamics was full of yet unexplored problems with wide ranges of opportunity for research initiative. When I began the work, I didn't at all expect that within a few months my experiments would yield such abundant results. In less than a year I published more than ten articles and presented lectures at several conferences.

In early 1962 I defended a dissertation on turbulent magnetohydrodynamic flows at the Moscow Institute of Aviation. I was spending more and more time at the Academy. I was becoming acquainted with more and more dignitaries of the scientific world of Moscow and Leningrad.

In connection with my work I had to read not only about hydrodynamics, but also about various fields of physics and astro-physics. All this brought me back again to an analysis of the mission and limitations of the natural sciences. I contrasted and compared "world culture and science" with the teaching of my people, illustrious figures of science with the sages and luminaries of Judaism.

I was drawing closer and closer to formulating my own unified world outlook. But it was necessary to collect and systematize my disparate thoughts, to make a written account of my philosophy. On one hand I didn't have time to do this, and on the other it was a pity to write something only to burn it or to bury it in the basement to be ruined by dampness. It seemed quite risky to keep at home manuscripts full of disproof of Leninism, now that at the insistence of the director I had become a regular employee of the Physics Institute, which was cooperating with security-cleared facilities. It seemed especially risky when my Polish escapade was taken into consideration, as well as my participation in pro-Israel evenings, my working at Rumbula and going to the synagogue on Saturdays.

In early 1963 I broke my leg and found myself on a forced leave of absence for several months. At that time the temptation to pour out the fruits of my many years of reflections finally won out.

I wrote night and day, crossing out, tearing up what was written and writing again. I finished all the work in a few weeks. When I had almost finished writing, we received notice that one of my relatives living in Tel Aviv was intending to come for a visit. Soon we learned that a relative from Fania's side was also coming, later. The prospect of meeting with Israelis, relatives at that, was very exciting. But as all my thoughts were riveted on my manuscript, the temptation overcame me to make use of the coming visits to send it to Israel. Just the thought of it made my heart stop beating. My reverence toward the Holy Land and everything connected to it was immeasurable. Religiously I collected not only stamps and postcards from Israel, but even candy wrappers which accidentally fell into my hands. And now suddenly it became possible that my beloved, long-nurtured creation could reach the Promised Land! Copying my work into a thick notebook, I waited eagerly for the relatives to arrive.

21 And so the quintessence of years of searching, doubting and transcending life-long prejudices found independent existence in the form of a thick notebook with a dark-blue leatherette cover, filled with fine handwriting. The main question to which I addressed myself was the truth or falseness of the thesis that the brilliant modern natural sciences and technology disprove and preclude religious faith.

From early childhood, long before I became fascinated by physics and even before my familiarity with Darwinism turned into zealous belief in evolution, I had assumed this thesis to be self-evident. All the people around me, of all ages and walks of life, regardless of their level of education or station in society, adamantly accepted this thesis as true. Whether staunch Communists or former sympathizers who had become literally fed-up with Communism (as was more often the case), the people around me all concurred in the belief that atheism is both inevitable and necessary "in our enlightened times." Yet no one bothered to think about the origin of this blind belief. No one was ready to go to the trouble of finding out whether this belief was justified. Although so many of the concepts and theses of Communism had turned out to be nonsense when applied to life, it did not occur to anyone to question the notorious thesis that science replaces religion.

It is interesting to note that at the time when I was writing all this, I did not yet know that Ben Gurion had often claimed that "science makes us atheists." Not only had he often repeated this wretched thesis, but he constructed the State of Israel and its system of public education upon its basis.

The first goal of my philosophical study was to explain how modern man forms a world outlook which leads him on to blind atheism and materialism. Examining the various methods of how consciousness is formed in my contemporaries, I reached the conclusion that materialism and atheism are foisted upon us. Most people are brainwashed into becoming materialistic atheists from a very young age, through their upbringing and education and never make any effort to ascertain the truth. But as even the most conditioned and submissive human mind nevertheless retains a minimal amount of curiosity, sufficient to ask a question or two, the initiation into atheism occurs simultaneously with the deification of science.

"Science has proven that . . ." sounds so solid, so imposing, so comfortable, so contemporary and useful in building up our self-satisfaction as representatives of this enlightened age. It does not matter if one never actually studied science or if one studied some years ago merely to pass exams and then forgot it. It does not matter that one has no idea about religion when he renounces it. All that matters for modern man is that science exists and scientists exist who have studied everything and know everything and have answered all the questions.

My second goal was to show what the natural sciences *can do* and what they *cannot do* because of the limits of their very essence. Here I had to investigate how the basic assumptions of any given science and thus the subsequent results of this science and the world picture it provides correspond to the real world.

The most important point for me to prove was that no science is capable of even touching upon the *essence* of things. Using symbols made to correspond to actual objects, science can study interactions between things. Science can make generalizations from the *phenomena* in which these things function. But it can never answer questions like "What *is* object *x*? What is its purpose?" (questions the answers to which are given solely through Divine revelation).

Then I further demonstrated how and why these and other limitations of science do not prevent it from succeeding when applied to practical use. In exactly the same way our orientation in the world and the actions we perform in it do not alter the fact that we have absolutely no concept of what lies behind the sensual images through which we perceive the material world around us and our own corporeal envelope.

While analyzing the question of the objectiveness of our perceptions, I was struck by the revelation that the very essence of philosophical materialism spells out its own obvious disproof. The materialist theory of cognition, which categorically claims that the universe can be known, is based upon the assumption that the aggregate of our sensory organs gives us a true picture of the world. In other words, the materialist theory of knowledge maintains that the human senses enable us to know the world "as it really is." Such shortsightedness! This claim categorically requires the acknowledgment of the existence of a Higher Power, a Supreme Arbiter, Who knows for sure "how the world really is" and can pit our partial knowledge against His absolute knowledge! Thus the fundamental premise of dialectical materialism inevitably leads to the recognition of the existence of God!

A large part of my essays was devoted to dispelling the artificial aureole surrounding the hypnotizing concepts of "science" and "scientists." In reality the craft of the scientist is in principle no different from that of a shoemaker, although the former is unquestionably more complex, requiring much more training. This is why the instruments, equations and terminology used by the craftsman of science being so incomprehensible to the layman are dazzling him into relating to the scientist as to a priest in a neo-pagan cult. Not only dilettantes, philistines and laymen fall prey to worshipping the seeming all-powerfulness of science, but also many scientists blindly believe that their research brings them closer to knowing the world and themselves.

In my writings I did not attempt to explain the Torah because I myself at the time had barely been able to scratch its surface and to sense, with the heart more than with the mind, its greatness and all-embracing significance. All I could do was to try to knock down the ridiculous stone wall erected by "enlighteners" which cuts us off from the treasures of the Torah and from God Himself.

This mental wall induces people to exclaim: "In our day and age one cannot believe that the world has been in existence for only five thousand years!" or: "You can't possibly believe — in the twentieth century — that whether or not I turn on the television on the Sabbath affects the fate of the Jewish people!" or: "How can an enlightened human being today say that God created man out of the dust of the earth or that He dictated the Torah to Moses on Mount Sinai?" Talking in this vein, pleased with their ultra-enlightenment, people fritter their lives away on nonsense at breakneck speed. Euphorically drifting into the abyss of irreversible assimilation and propelling their children in the same direction, they dauntlessly flit past the eternal truth and the eternal values kept by Jews for centuries.

The sum total of my notes constituted a kind of "preparing

of the ground," clearing away atheistic rubbish and "enlightened" gibberish from the building site. Only after having done this was it possible to begin rebuilding the house with a Jewish world outlook. At this culminating point, I called upon my imaginary reader (or, to be more exact, myself, now freed of prejudices) to open the Book of Books—the source and repository of our distinctiveness and eternalness. I called upon him/myself to trust in the truths that have not been influenced by time, to learn them and to rise to the ultimate affirmation of Judaism — *Shema Yisrael!*

22   I won't attempt to describe the excitement of my Israeli uncle's visit. Concerning my manuscript, though, my relative, guided by worldly wisdom befitting his age, said that it seemed to him a risk involving possible unpleasant consequences for me far greater than what the situation warranted. Painfully, I came to agree.

By the time that Fania's relative arrived, I had devised a new plan for transporting the manuscript. I reached the conclusion that the safest and most hopeful way was for her to pass it on to the Israeli Embassy during her stay in Moscow.

Pecking with one finger on the keys of the typewriter, I typed out the manuscript onto the thinnest paper. Now it could all fit into a regular postal envelope.

Fania and I scheduled our vacations to begin when her relative was to arrive. After receiving our guest in Riga, the two of us traveled to Moscow a few days before she joined us there.

In Moscow we visited Fania's relative several times at her hotel, where we held discussions on the most harmless, neutral subjects. Once, when she went out to the street with us to bid us farewell, I arranged to meet her at the large pharmacy on the Twenty-Fifth of October Street. The rendezvous was kept. I explained my request to her. She agreed and took the manuscript. The next day the manuscript was delivered to the Embassy.

It all went simply and smoothly. It ought to have stopped right there, but a thirst for further meetings with Israelis possessed me. Possibly, this thirst was aroused by a feeling of some sort of disappointment left by the encounters that had just taken place. Although by that time I was quite well read and informed about life in Israel, nevertheless I expected Israeli Jews to be surrounded by a halo of holiness or at least a sign of the Chosen People. Their behavior, their mode of thinking, their interests should set them apart from all other peoples. Alas, this was not so. I convinced myself that those with whom I had become acquainted were not characteristic representatives.

I had heard that many foreigners frequented the Aragvi restaurant in Moscow. In the evening of the same day that my manuscript had made it to the Embassy, we went to that restaurant. I was already not eating anything at places like that, but for appearances I ordered something and persistently pecked my fork on the plate. And suddenly—my heart missed a beat. The two couples occupying the neighboring table were speaking loudly in Hebrew. On the coats of the men were little badges with blue stars of David.

I did not dare start to talk to them in the restaurant in front of everybody. Therefore I decided that we should wait until they finished dining, and then we would meet them on the street.

While they were finishing their meal, we hastily paid and dashed into the street. I was terribly excited. Soon they also left. We said "shalom" and asked them in Hebrew if they were Israeli tourists. It turned out that they were not tourists but workers at the Embassy. This made the meeting even more interesting, but, of course, more risky. They asked us to join them. It was almost midnight and Gorky Street was quite deserted. The warm, windless night, saturated with the aroma of flowering linden trees, evoked tranquility, but inside me everything seethed with excitement. Just think of it: me strolling along the center of Moscow with an Israeli diplomat!

One of them, Moshe Z., gently led me by the arm and answered the countless questions that erupted from me. Fania was walking behind us with the second diplomat and both wives. I asked Moshe about the spiritual condition in Israel, about the education of children, and about many, many other things.

It disturbed me a little that half an hour earlier, as I had seen with my own eyes, the entire company had eaten the most non-kosher dishes with tremendous appetite. But I tried not to think about this.

I told Moshe that I had passed my precious manuscript on to the Embassy and asked him to keep an eye on its fate.

Meanwhile Fania said that I very much wanted to have a *Chumash* and *machzorim* with Russian translation. They promised her to bring all this to the synagogue on Arkhipova Street on the coming Saturday. This again puzzled me, as I already knew that it is forbidden to carry things on Shabbath.

When we mentioned that from Moscow we were going on to Transcaucasia to spend the rest of our vacation there, our new friends announced that they were also leaving for vacation in a few days — to Yalta in the Crimea. They suggested that we travel to Transcaucasia via Crimea so that we could see each other again. It was best and safest to meet and talk on the beach — they explained — where it is always full of people in bathing suits, making it difficult for anyone to notice or recognize us.

23 On Shabbath at the synagogue I received a *tallith* and books from the Embassy employees, as had been arranged.

Now it remained for us to decide whether to go to Yalta. We soberly deemed it to be folly, but the temptation was so great that we decided to go.

Fania was four months pregnant and felt ill traveling. Arriving in Yalta, we launched a desperate attempt to get a hotel room, but this, of course, was impossible. Then I decided to call the hotel for foreign tourists, the Ukrainia, where the Z's had to be staying. I called there anyway, not even hoping that it would work, but surprisingly it turned out that it was possible to get a "deluxe" room for two days.

It was clear that after all my former contacts and with my present work, it was forbidden for us to go to this hotel. But Fania was barely able to stand on her feet, so I decided to disregard all our fears.

The next day I caught the Z's on the hotel stairs, and we agreed to meet on the "Golden Beach" during the following day. We spent a few happy hours with the Z's that day, talking, looking at Israeli postcards. In parting, I wrote down and gave them our address and the addresses of our relatives in Israel.

When we returned to the hotel, I noticed two young men near the manager's desk. At first glance they didn't please me very much.

That evening we sailed by ship to Sukhumi. Those fellows from the hotel, however, haunted us for a long time, serving as food for all kinds of conjectures and not very pleasant suppositions.

I met the Z's two more times in Russia. Each time I tried to find out what was happening with my manuscript, but they didn't know. The first time was at a concert of the Israeli pianist Pnina Saltzman in Leningrad. The second was at an international film festival in Moscow where the Israeli film *Remember* was also shown. I should note that the film depressed me, not only by its mediocrity but even more by its blasphemous presentation of memories of the horrors of Nazi concentration camps against the background of scenes of a Jew living together with his French concubine in contemporary Israel.

At Sukhumi, I also became close friends with a family of Georgian Jews named Krikheli. In the coming years I visited them a few times during the high holy days of Rosh Hashana and Yom Kippur, in order to spend these days in Jewish surroundings and to go to the synagogue without fear.

Still, the manuscript was there, in Israel, and this heartened and quieted me. Even the thought that it was possible that I was condemned to remain until the end of my days on alien soil seemed less frightening. After all, a small part of me was already in the Holy Land.

24   I continued to go regularly to the synagogue on Shabbath mornings. Sometimes, as before, I stood alone in the rear corner of the large upstairs hall, but more and more I preferred to go down to the basement to the Chassidim. There my place was between two pensioners—Shmuel-Aaron Raphelson, who first taught me how to find my way in the prayer book, in order to find the place in the text at any given moment, and the late Nochem Besser, who patiently answered my countless questions about Judaism, one more naïve than the other. Besser, as I found out later, secretly taught Torah and *halacha* to dozens of boys and girls. These magnificent, shy and good men rendered me a priceless service in my search for Judaism, and I am infinitely grateful to them.

One Shabbath at the beginning of 1964 a forty-year-old man approached me. He had a black moustache and extraordinarily lively, pure-blue eyes with a glint of mischief in them. Vigor and inspiration brimmed in him. He started to insist that I come with him to his house, promising to tell me many important and interesting things and to give me good Jewish books. Right there he wanted to know if I put on *tefillin* daily. As I didn't know what that was, he insisted even more that I come over. As he went away he suggested that I find out about him from any of the synagogue congregants, as "everyone knows who Notke with the moustache is."

He left me with mixed feelings. First of all, I was not accustomed to Jewish books being offered in public, in the presence of witnesses. This involuntarily alarmed me and forced me to query if he were a provocateur. On the other hand, there was something very attractive about him.

I asked Raphelson about Notke and he replied: "He's a Chassid. You can go with him."

I wondered what "Chassid" meant. Wasn't that section of the synagogue called "Chassidim"? However, I was ashamed to ask. Thus, the gradations and nuances of the concept of "Chassid," nay the very concept, remained an enigma to me for a long time to come.

In March, nine days before Pesach, a son was born to us. We gave him a double name, Hertz-Daniel. The first name was in memory of my father, and the second one pleased Fania very much. The functionary at the "Bureau of Registration of Acts of Civilian Status" point-blank refused to register a double name. It didn't help either appealing to a superior authority or attesting, among other things, that the Azerbaijanis register four or five names, plus their invariable "ogli" at the end.

The boy was registered under the name Hertz. We started to call him Geka for short. But, naturally, at the circumcision we gave him both names.

The day before the circumcision I went to invite Notke. This was an appropriate occasion to take advantage of his offer finally. However, for some reason he could not come. When the baby was almost a month old, Nochem Besser told me about the *pidyon ha'ben* ritual — the symbolic redemption of a first-born son from a *kohen*, a member of the priestly class. For this purpose he advised me to invite Notke, who was a *kohen*.

This custom seemed strange to me, possibly even absurd. Wonderfully enough, though, I had felt nothing of the kind in relation to the ceremony of circumcision. Such is human nature that the unfamiliar seems foolish and wild. Restraining my doubts, however, I invited Notke and Besser, and everything went according to *halacha*.

From then on Notke masterfully plunged into our life, often evoking the displeasure of Fania for "pushing" too much. Looking back in retrospect now, I feel tremendous gratitude towards Notke, just as I was then irrepressibly pulled toward him. He symbolized for me the quintessence of Judaism, the Torah, the Jewish way of life. Through Notke's mediation, a perfectly new world was opened up to me. Furthermore, he was a most outstanding personality, even though from the point of view of the social circle to which we belonged, he was a simple, uneducated Jew.

I was amazed at the integrity of his world outlook and the uncompromising agreement between his behavior and this world outlook.

It was a joy to see a man who was very earthy, loving all that was beautiful and savory, yet nevertheless always inspired by an ideal. He was not suffering for his ideal. He hated sacrifice. It was just that he simply could not conceive of himself outside the constant awareness of and adherence to this ideal. Therefore having to forgo something was not a sacrifice but the only possible natural way to behave.

Notke did many things daily that the average philistine would consider an unbearable burden and an enormous sacrifice to personal comfort. It amazed me that this man, without having completed high school, was able to talk for hours about philosophical difficulties in explaining the creation of matter *ex nihilo*, about time as one of the dimensions of the physical world, about the Divine soul of the Jew, and about the necessity for that soul to master and control the body, which ought not to be rejected but rather ennobled through keeping the commandments.

Once I asked him how he had arrived at all this, and he burst out laughing in reply. "I don't make this up by myself. It's all written."

"Where?"

"Here at least, in this book that I study." He showed me a pocket-sized book. "This is *Tanya*, the major book of the Old Rebbe."

"And you studied it?"

"No. I *am* learning it."

"For how long?"

"For a few decades."

This was very strange to me, used to studying several volumes in the course of a few weeks or even days in preparation for each one of the numerous exams which I had taken in my life.

Often Notke referred to the *Kabbala*, to the *Zohar*. I admit that this frightened me and made me uncomfortable. The fact was that I had never read or even seen the books of the *Zohar*. However, I remembered a few allusions to the *Kabbala* in Shalom Aleichem, particularly in his story "Song of Songs." From these I concluded that the *Kabbala* was a collection of very primitive, childishly naïve mystical tales.

Things got even harder, especially when Notke "pushed" me to fulfill a few commandments that I had never heard of before. Already on one of my first visits he had presented me with a little velvet bag of *tefillin*, insisting that I put them on right there and then under his guidance and direction. He explained that these phylacteries had to be put on every morning except on Shabbath and holidays.

To tell the truth, it was very difficult for me to do this. Thousands of voices inside of me began to screech and resist. All that I had internalized from Soviet education shrieked: "No!" All that had sunk into my brain from Soviet universities howled: "Never!" All that had been absorbed in me from my atheistic surroundings revolted and protested: "This is primitive!"

True, I had already gone far in rejecting my past education and in adopting Judaism. But for me Judaism still seemed to be food for the soul and the mind, a sublime philosophical system. So suddenly being confronted with such material, physical duties was most strange for me. True also, I had long since understood and accepted many commandments relating to the sphere of everyday and physical things, such as kosher food, many of the Sabbath laws, circumcision and so forth. Yet, I had been familiar with these for a long time and understood them without reflection. The commandment of *tefillin*, however, was unknown and seemed very strange. The dictum of the Pentateuch that "... thou shalt bind them for a sign upon thine hand, and they shall be for frontlets between thine eyes..." I was inclined to interpret purely allegorically.

The fact was that I did not only not know the practice and meaning of the Oral Law which elucidates the Pentateuch, but I didn't even suspect that it existed. Nevertheless, Notke's insistence and even more so a deeper internal voice compelled me to continue the daily practice of the commandment of putting on *tefillin*. I very soon started to feel extremely uneasy, to suffer from a strong sensation of non-fulfillment and of spiritual defection, if for any reason I did not manage to put on *tefillin* in the morning.

A month after I had first put on *tefillin*, I had to go to Leningrad for a conference. I arrived there by train early in the morning and rushed immediately to the synagogue where I could perform this *mitzva*. But to my extreme disappointment, I found the synagogue already closed. So instead of attending the conference for which I had come, I spent the whole day trying to get a place in a hotel, where I could put on my *tefillin*. Neither persuasion nor bribery could help. I didn't eat anything all day, and I shivered terribly as I ran in the cruel frost from one hotel to another. But I was unaware of all this against the background of my great distress that the sun was declining lower and lower while I still had not put on *tefillin*. Miraculously, I somehow obtained a cherished key three minutes before the sun set and managed after all to do this daily obligation. What kind of irrational power controlled me that day? What had become of my scientific skepticism?

Similar experiences occurred with other *mitzvoth*. For example, during the first days after I started to wear a *tallith katan* with *tzitzith* tassels on the corners, I simply felt like a clown, even though the *tzitzith* were carefully tucked under my clothes and nobody saw them. However, after a month this feeling became entirely reversed. Without *tzitzith* I simply felt naked. Sometimes, due to my absent-mindedness, these tassels would stick out from under my clothes. My colleagues at the Academy of Sciences on occasion would snatch the *tzitzith* and ask in astonishment what they were or if I wore underwear that was so threadbare that the threads were unraveling.

In the manuscript sent to Israel I had tried to convince both myself and others of the vital necessity to fulfill all the commandments of the Torah. Now I was enduring psychological difficulties in trying to actually practice what I had preached. How trying it was for Fania then, who at best was a benevolent reader of my essays! Suddenly she was confronted with a kosher kitchen and Shabbath candles, Shabbath rest, as well as monthly immersion in the *mikveh* . . .

Albeit with hardship, the eternal triumphed over the superficial and the alien. The more I entered into this new life, the more I felt myself participating in the mission of my people. The bits of knowledge from the Torah which previously had been known to me became lit with new understanding. At that time more and more treasures appeared on my horizons — the commentaries of Rashi, the *Mishna,* the *Shulchan Aruch.* The Talmud at that time still remained closed to me, but I managed to extract grains of information about it through quotations or references in other books.

25 ██ Finally the day came when I felt able to study Torah independently. A wonderful period began — a time of cognition, re-evaluation and daily discovery.

On the surface, my life continued as usual. There was the trip every morning to the Institute of Physics at the Academy of Sciences, followed by long hours in the laboratory with endless discussions of the latest experimental results. There would be agonizing searches to find the reasons for the failure of a test that had been repeated over and over again. And there was always work with PhD students and participation in scientific conferences.

As usual, books filled with formulas and schematics found their way to my desk at home. Scattered piles of written papers grew almost up to the ceiling. Some of these papers were filed, but most of them ended up in the waste basket. But in the midst of this stream of papers, the *Chumash*, the *Mishna*, the *Shulchan Aruch* and of course *Tanya* now invariably remained on my desk. Putting aside the hand-written pages, immediately forgetting the despicably vain attempts of human intellect reflected in them, I could plunge into the pure, life-giving, tranquil yet passionate ocean of eternal wisdom.

Gradually and very cautiously Notke introduced me to his circle of friends. I became acquainted with self-controlled and always externally calm Yisroel Pevzner, with temperamental Shimon Gutman. For several months I studied Torah with Rashi's commentary with Avroam Godin, who before the Second World War had been the secretary of none other than Mordechai Dubin, who for years had represented the entire Jewish community to the Latvian government. With respect I observed Mordechai Aharon Friedman — a man of Biblical appearance — whose seniority, erudition and invincible will enjoyed indisputable authority among the Chassidim of Riga.

All his friends were as dedicated as Notke himself. For all of them, compromise or accommodation to the Soviet reality at the expense of disobeying the *Shulchan Aruch* was not just inadmissible but simply didn't exist as a possible alternative.

They searched for Jewish children who showed interest in Judaism and tried to help them. This was such an important thing to Notke and his friends that for its sake they would forget about food and drink. Under their influence, many elderly people — who when younger had been able to learn Torah and Hebrew — were transformed into secret teachers for these children. For security reasons they never taught more than one child at a time, but as most of them were pensioners with free time available, they had a total of many students.

How can we measure the contribution of these modest anonymous people to the awakening of Soviet Jewry? I have already mentioned Nochem Besser. Another indefatigable teacher was Gradus, whose first name I have unfortunately forgotten. This shy, small man feared neither hard frost nor Soviet law as he tirelessly treaded from house to house. Alas, he is no longer alive. His dream of going to Israel, which he had cherished so, was never realized. There are many others who are still alive and working. May their days be increased!

The dwellings of the Chassidim (which often were only single rooms within large communal apartments) were clear of all Soviet influence. Their children and grandchildren breathed, from infancy, love and devotion for the Jewish people and the Torah. They all lived in the hope of leaving for *Eretz Hakodesh*. They had absolutely no doubt about either the necessity or the hoped-for realization of this departure. Some sort of secret surrounded them that was greater than simply a conspiracy. I felt that there was a side of their life still beyond my comprehension. This feeling was confirmed all the more when I found out that every one of them contributed at least a fifth of his sometimes very modest income to a charity fund.

My donations were also accepted, but where they went remained a mystery to me. Only much later did they tell me of the existence in those years of a secret system of Jewish education and training which helped many children return and stay in the fold of Judaism. Even now it would be premature to openly discuss in more detail the hundreds of miniature *yeshivoth* and *chadorim* spread all over immense Russia. Hidden in private apartments, these institutions operated under the strictest secrecy regulations which became an easy, matter-of-fact routine for both pupils and teachers. During the Stalin era, punishment in case of discovery was death; later it was reduced to "years." But none of the participants in this underground educational movement was thwarted by this danger.

Many things distinguished my new friends from my nationalistically and Zionistically inclined acquaintances: their integrity, their deep knowledge of the Torah, their lively wisdom, their clear conception of the meaning and purpose of life. Their trustworthiness was self-evident. It would be simply inconceivable to suspect treachery or K.G.B. collaboration in someone who, in the name of the Jewish ideal, against a great many objective difficulties, brought each of his own steps into conformity with Jewish learning and built on this a life for all generations of his family.

The fruits of their efforts were felt. They believed it was most important for a Jew to remain a genuine Jew and to help others return to Judaism. Wherever fate may have thrust them, they knew how to bring this about. Their desire to go to Israel flowed out of their world outlook, naturally and organically.

Finally, I found out that they have a spiritual leader, a rebbe. He was not only their leader, but the great Jew of the entire generation, the preceptor of all Jews, in that he taught and urged the need to study Torah more deeply and more scrupulously, to fulfill the commandments with a great spiritual uplift, and to educate oneself and one's children to love every Jew as one in whom a portion of the Lord resides. I discovered that the Rebbe is called the Lubavitcher from the name of the small town of Lubavitch in White Russia. My new friends were correspondingly Lubavitcher Chassidim, also called Chabad Chassidim from the first letters of three concepts: *chochma* — wisdom, reason; *bina* — comprehension; *da'ath* — knowledge. These were the three essential elements in the philosophical teaching of this branch of Chassidism. I discovered more and more the unusual life strength and steadiness of Chabad both as a teaching and as a movement. The terrible millstones of the Cheka, G.P.U., N.K.V.D., M.G.B., K.G.B., names of Soviet secret police, and the Soviet propaganda apparatus which for fifty years had been crushing all and sundry seemed powerless to crush Chabad, although for a time it acted against it especially violently.

I became acquainted with many illustrious Chabadniks and heard amazing stories about others. These were extraordinary people — earthy, not self-denying. Thanks to a confluence of unshakable belief and a clear world outlook guiding their behavior, they were able to overcome insurmountable obstacles. I almost never heard them complaining about the difficulties facing Jews in the Soviet Union trying to keep the Jewish way of life. With their mood permanently elevated, they unequivocally reasoned that if the Almighty gave us the *Shulchan Aruch* — the Jewish Code — then He certainly also provided us with the means to obey it, regardless of the external circumstances. And miraculously enough, this approach, based on absolute *bitachon ba-Shem*, always won against all odds.

I heard about the legendary Mendel Futerfas, who rescued thousands of Jews from Soviet captivity. He himself remained inside the Soviet Union until after the completion of this unbelievable act. Then he was captured and condemned to death. While waiting for the execution of his sentence, he sat in solitary confinement and sang Russian folk songs, which he carefully chose and imbued with deep allegorical meaning. They commuted his sentence to twenty-five years, but after ten years he was able to leave Russia and now lives in Israel.

I heard about Chaim Zalman Kozliner, nicknamed "Chazak" (Strong). When N.K.V.D. agents came to arrest him, he raised his arms and began to chant words from the *Kabbala* with such strength of feeling that the police retreated.

I became acquainted with Schneer Pinsky. The tiny Moscow apartment of this small, quiet man served as both a shelter and an academy of Chassidism for scores of Jewish visitors from all corners of Russia.

Wherever I would travel, whether to capital cities or to remote corners, if there were any vestiges of Yiddishkeit—a *minyan* praying regularly, a *mikveh* still providing ritual ablution, a *melamed* still teaching children, a *sukka* still being built for the autumn holiday of *Sukkoth*—investigation revealed that all this was maintained by one or two "possessed" Chabadniks. Sometimes, even, the Chabadnik had left the area ten or so years before, but the order established by him was still functioning. This was repeated in Russia, Belorussia, the Transcaucasus and Central Asia.

26

Outwardly, our life changed rather little. I continued to work at the Physics Institute. My experiments on magnetohydrodynamics were progressing very successfully. I studied the influence of the magnetic field on turbulent flows of liquid metals and electrolytes. This was then a totally unknown area. When I could ascertain which research methods should be applied, after having overcome an entire set of difficulties, I felt like a traveler on a mountain road where after every curve, after every new pass, new horizons and perspectives were opened up.

Though, of course, from a philosophical point of view I harbored no illusions about the significance of my work, I must admit that on the whole it pleased me. I published much, participated in conferences and had undergraduate and graduate students. But real life began only on those rare, meaningful evenings when I managed to get to the Chassidic lessons on Torah. Most of the day I spent in the "scientific world." I had occasion to meet with many professors and academicians, who five or so years before seemed to me to be standing on pedestals of inaccessible height. Now I had the occasion to observe them close up. Some of them were still modest. Others put on airs. But when I compared them to those who study Torah — who, as I now understood, really deserve the name scholar, although having neither title nor rank — all these professors seemed to me to be pitiful pygmies. The fact was that not only were most of them possessed by all possible passions and ambitions, but that science and the social status conferred by it were, to a great degree, means of satisfying these lusts. Even those who were sincerely dedicated to their science now seemed to me to be limited in comparison to the bearded Jew, who, although having never completed any university, penetrates into the very meaning of the essence of the universe through reading an ancient volume in a sing-song voice.

Not long before, the path of human history had seemed to me to be marked by the milestones of scientific and technological achievements. Now I distinctly saw and even more strongly felt that this history is unwinding according to the eternal and invariable plan set down in the Torah. Technical progress receded to the very bottom of the scale of genuine values.

My double life demanded great effort and maximum economy of time. Even previously I had never known what boredom from lack of activity was. I never understood how some people have to rack their brains to figure out how to "kill time." During my student days while associating with fellow students or while traveling by train, whenever I would allow myself to be persuaded to be drawn into a game, I would suffer deeply and wait for the moment that I would finally be released from this vacuous pastime. At such times I would always have the feeling of participating in a premeditated crime of reducing down to nothing the most precious and wondrous gift — time, intended for construction, creation and the striving for self-perfection. Now, after my encounter with Torah and commandments the appreciation of time became even stronger.

27 After meeting with the people from the Israeli Embassy and forwarding my manuscript, I constantly felt that I was being followed. As I didn't notice anything positively suspicious, I tried to convince myself that this was merely the fruit of my active imagination. However, in the end I came to be convinced that my intuition was not deceiving me.

After our baby was born, I finally received an apartment from the Academy in the "academic settlement" of Salaspils, twenty-three kilometers east of Riga. The entire settlement consisted at that time of a few four-storey brick houses. Two kilometers away an experimental atomic reactor belonging to my Institute was already functioning. There the building where the magnetohydrodynamics laboratories of Riga were to be transferred was also being erected. In the meantime I commuted to Riga to work. Fania was working at the Institute of Organic Synthesis, also in Riga. My mother would come every day to the baby, but the trip, the walk and taking care of the child were taxing her strength. Therefore we searched persistently for a suitable nursemaid. Our happiness was boundless when we finally found a poor old woman who lived nearby. She stayed alone with the child all day. Before leaving the house in the morning I would carefully hide, beneath my underwear, my *tefillin*, *tallith* and the few Jewish books which I had.

One morning, just as I arrived at work, the telephone rang.

"Is Branover at work today?"

I recognized the voice of the directress of the personnel department.

"This is Branover. What's the matter?" As I answered I immediately felt anxious.

"No, no. Everything's all right. Someone here asked for you. They'll call you." She was evidently in a hurry to hang up.

It was obvious: they wanted to be certain that I hadn't stayed home for any reason. (Later, in the evening, I found out that the same thing had happened to Fania at work, but she hadn't paid any attention to it.)

The next train to Salaspils left only an hour later. That hour dragged out agonizingly. On the way home I tried to convince myself that my imagination was simply playing tricks on me. Nevertheless I ran home from the station. A gray Pobeda parked near the house neighboring ours, immediately drew my attention. Running up the stairs, I silently opened the door, entered the little anteroom and froze.

The door to the next room was closed. From behind it I could hear male voices. I should have stood and listened, but my nerves couldn't take it. I flung open the door.

Geka was peacefully playing on the floor. Seeing me, he started smiling and crawled to meet me. To the side stood three men talking to our nursemaid.

"What's the matter?" I asked.

"It doesn't concern you," one of them answered. "We had some questions to ask your employee. Please excuse us that we had to talk to her in your apartment."

They left almost immediately, taking the old woman with them. The next day she came and said that she refused to work for us.

There was no doubt now that we were being followed. It worried me greatly that they probably knew that I had passed something on to the Israeli Embassy. Although I was not officially connected with any secret work, I was surrounded by people and entire laboratories connected with various military departments studying questions related to rockets, submarines and so forth. If they wished, the K.G.B. could easily accuse me of transmitting secret information to Israel and do with me as they pleased.

Half a year went by before the assistant director of the Institute summoned me. He then contended that I was receiving packages "from the West." I truly had not received anything and therefore was quite sincerely filled with indignation. However, he stood his ground, reprimanding: "You must understand where you are working. If you were working at the Loggers' Authority, then you could receive all the packages you pleased." Arguing with him was just as impossible as with the characters at the K.G.B.

Finally, a year later, I was called to the "Special Department" of the Academy. I was most courteously requested to meet at my convenience with one of their members, who wished to talk to me.

The meeting took place the next day. My interlocutor showed me his permit. Written there was: "Committee of State Security, Chief of the Department — Coleman."

"Please tell me about all your meetings with foreigners," he asked with great gentility.

I tried to tell him about meetings with my first cousin once removed who had come from Israel two years before to visit and about some other chance encounters on the street. It was clear, however, what he was driving at.

"Please try a little harder," he insisted. Then his voice became cruel and inexorable. "Remember that your fate is being decided at this moment."

I continued to persist. Then he told me — in excruciating detail — about my meetings in Moscow on Gorky Street and in Yalta, where on the beach I wrote something on a piece of paper torn from a green notebook and gave it to employees of the Israeli Embassy.

"What was it?" he insisted.

"The address of my uncle and of my brother-in-law's second cousin in Israel. I asked to send them regards," I answered.

For several hours this idiotic dialogue was repeated over and over. When it got very late, he let me go, ordering me to come again in the morning.

At night I calmed down. Considering everything, I came to the conclusion that two years of checking apparently had convinced them that there were no really serious charges against me, and they were probably not interested in "blowing up" the matter just then. (Still, for security reasons, I curtailed my visits with Notke.)

Later I found out that the director of the Institute had insistently kept me from being kicked out.

28 Gradually I began to renew my visits to Notke and my Chassidic activities. Especially moving were the Chassidic evening gatherings — *farbrengen* — and their way of celebrating the major holidays. Forty to fifty people would get together, including newcomers to Judaism. Most of these gatherings took place in the autumn and winter, and now that I look back upon them the image that comes to mind is the striking contrast between the coldness and darkness outside and the warmth and light inside the room throbbing with excited people.

But stronger than the physical contrast was the psychological contrast. People came and went one at a time as a security precaution. But once they were inside, the K.G.B. and the Soviet regime ceased to exist for them. They became free and independent participants in something grand and eternal, subject only to the Almighty.

They sang heartening Chassidic melodies — with words and without words. Some of them were like genuine symphonies, full of feeling and philosophical reflections. Everyone felt bound to one another by the *mitzva* of love for the People of Israel, for the Holy Land and for one's fellow Jew. This *mitzva* was fully carried out on these holidays taking place in praise of the Almighty and under His protection. During festive meals, with tears in their eyes, people would wish one another a speedy departure for Israel. Then the readings would begin. They read *ma'amarim* — the writings of the Rebbe.

It was hard for me to understand these *ma'amarim* and to follow the stormy discussions. I was restricted by my lack of knowledge of the language, consisting of a combination of Hebrew and Aramaic and also by the abundance of references to the Talmud, the Zohar, the Rambam and so forth. They also read *sichoth* — speeches of the Rebbe in Yiddish, and these were easier to understand, as I had picked up quite a bit of Yiddish from my friendship and studies with the Chassidim.

I never ceased to be amazed at the philosophic and psychological depth of the Rebbe's thought and at the strength of his foresight. Later I tried to translate some of the *sichoth* into Russian so they could be accessible to the uninitiated. In particular one of the Rebbe's *sichoth* on Chanuka moved me and made a deep imprint on my mind.

In it the question is asked why — out of all the events commemorated by Chanuka — does the Talmud single out precisely the seemingly modest episode of the jug of oil for the Temple lamps rather than the mighty military victories of the Maccabees over the Greeks? The Rebbe explains that the oil for the Temple lamps symbolizes wisdom. Just as the Greeks profaned the oil by their contact, so does the smallest exposure to non-Jewish influence always profane Jewish wisdom. There can be no compromise, not even the slightest adulteration in the sphere of the Jewish spirit!

It is also stated there that the world is constructed by the Creator so that, in the natural course of events, non-Jews simply should not rule over Jews, except in the case where . . . Jews give themselves and their Torah over to the control of non-Jews. It was very understandable to us since we in Soviet Russia experienced the consequences of allowing the gentiles in.

In another place the Rebbe said that it is not the possibility of *ge'ula* (redemption) that should seem unusual. On the contrary, the prolonged *galuth* (exile) should seem strange, surprising and unnatural. All this provided much food for thought and debate.

There were periods when I set up a strict schedule of Jewish studies for myself. Especially enthralling were the lessons on the *Tanya*, which Zalman Levin — a great, quiet man and a living encyclopedia of Judaism and Chassidism — gave me. Not long before, he had been released from prison after a ten-year confinement, during which he did not once eat non-kosher food or break the Shabbath. Now he was working as a craftsman-electrician at a factory. With his son, Moshe Chaim, I translated an abridged Russian version of the *Shulchan Aruch* — the code of Jewish laws. Naturally while we worked together Moshe Chaim and I talked a lot about Chassidism, especially about the *Tanya*.

It amazed me when I found more and more answers in the *Tanya* or in the other book of the Alter Rebbe — *Likutei Torah* — to questions that had been troubling me so many years. I found answers to questions about the spiritual and physical worlds; about the order of creation of the material world by God from nothing; about how universal preordainment from above still allows for man's free will and his freedom of choice. Principally I learned about the higher destination of man, how man can become spiritualized by permeating his life with Torah, without resorting to asceticism. The simple, refined and immeasurably profound teaching about the struggle of the Divine soul and the bestial soul within man gave me a completely new understanding of the concept of the Chosen People, of the commandment to love one's fellow Jew, and of various aspects of Jewish life and behavior. In contrast to this, how poor Freudian theory looked. Although of Jewish origin, Freud did not realize the prime aspect of man — the Divine spark.

Most difficult of all for me to understand and accept was the grandeur and profoundness of simplicity. As I have already said, as long as the Jewish religion and the Torah were identified in my mind as a system expressed in complex philosophical terms, then everything was all right. But crisis ensued when it became evident that the Torah is primarily a practical guide to everyday life and that the philosophy which permeates it is — both in essence and in form — absolutely unlike the university texts to which I was so accustomed.

In the textbooks everything was directed toward classification and generalization, toward showing similarities within outward differences and diversity. The Torah, on the contrary, primarily narrates things unique, exclusive and nonpareil: a chosen people — the Jews; a time set apart — the Shabbath; a land incomparable to any other place in the world — Israel, and its center — Jerusalem; and singular forefathers, holy men and prophets. And only in the One and only God is all the uniqueness universally generalized, and unified.

My intellect in no way could reconcile itself to this new seemingly "unscientific" way of looking at the world. It was even harder to accept the stories of the Torah about miracles, about supernatural events.

It took me years to understand that it was not at all modern "sophistication" or the "progress" of the human intellect that stood between me and the concept of miracles, but rather certain notions and ideas absorbed almost since infancy. Until now it had never seemed necessary to check, analyze or reconsider them.

According to these ideas, our age is a special age — the century of science. Mysticism is used as a derogatory term and belief in the supernatural is considered to be a sign of feeble-mindedness. Even much later, when I already understood that, in principle, science cannot contradict belief, and that the essence of things and the origin and development of the universe are absolutely out of the reach of science and represent an area where Torah rules supreme, still the question of miracles disturbed, troubled and frightened me. It took me even more time to realize the simple truth that someone living one or two thousand years ago and myself are in the very same position regarding miracles. A miracle is called a miracle precisely because it occurs so very rarely. Therefore, an ancient believer, just like myself, probably never saw a miracle occur. And also, just like me, he saw only the natural course of events united by bonds of cause and effect in everyday life.

Being a student of twentieth-century natural science based on indeterminism and probability physics, I should have had a more favorable attitude toward intelligently comprehending miracles. Unfortunately, my mind was constrained by an education and psychology invented by shortsighted, arrogant, lazy people at the dawn of the so-called "Age of Enlightenment."

My internal protest and rejection of the supernatural increased if the events in question took place in the recent past or present. My "intellectualizing" mind quietly accepted the idea of One Almighty God Who chose the Jewish People. But upon being presented with the situation that this Creator — Who granted the universe existence and definable laws — sometimes changes these laws for a definite purpose, my mind would become alarmed and discomforted. My intellect also rose up against the Chassidic acceptance of mind-reading and the prediction of the future by contemporary *tzaddikim*, against the idea of transmigration of souls, and against the type of dialogue with God and display of supernatural powers attributed to, for instance, the Ba'al Shem Tov.

It was enormously difficult for me to accept the idea of *hashgacha pratith* — that God exercises permanent supervision and control over all living beings and inanimate objects in the universe. Involuntarily attempting to imagine a human being in the role of such an overseer, our mind is convinced that such a person is impossible and hence concludes — completely contradicting elementary logic — that this is impossible for God also.

Curiously, our forefathers possessed a breadth of vision ample enough to contain a genuine idea of God. Yet, we who have been brought up in a world of man-made electronic computers which can supervise millions of objects at once — surely we ought to feel it easier to imagine the power of the Limitless Mighty One, but we don't!

The principle of continual creation formulated by the Ba'al Shem Tov helped me to overcome this difficulty. This principle affirms that God not only directs all things in the world, but is continuously creating them from non-existence, renewing their existence. And if this continual creation were to cease for an instant, then everything existing would turn into nothing. This principle is even more radical than that of Divine supervision, but, possibly, it is precisely this which makes it easier for a mind educated in rationalism to grasp.

As long as I was only reading the explanations of all these phenomena in the *Kabbala* or in the philosophy of Chabad, I felt totally at ease. The theory of the creation of matter from Divine emanation through successive contractions and abasement of the spiritual in favor of the material, as well as the principle of continual creation (which actually defined the possibility of the reverse influence of a righteous man upon the acts of creation by God) overwhelmed me by their rightness, wisdom and refinement.

However, when it came to applying these theories to life, a psychological barrier went into effect. The imprint of my atheistic upbringing and education was solidly lodged within me. Psychological habits turned out to be stronger than ideology and reason.

Many years passed until I could resign myself to intellectually accept and then to genuinely feel, on a higher level of consciousness, truths such as the idea that a righteous Jew putting on phylacteries can sometimes more successfully defend the Jewish people than an armada of tanks or an escadrille of airplanes. It is impossible to prove or disprove this, but within the framework of Jewish philosophy it can be explained. In order to become imbued with these convictions, one must stop resisting them and dwell for a while within their wonderful world. The extraordinarily harmonious and profound Chassidic principle of continual creation, of the provision of the universe with life energy, clearly and convincingly explains why the behavior of every single Jew, determines the fate of the world, since the amount of life energy is a function of this behavior.

But it is not enough to be intellectually elated by the harmony of the tenet of the origination of the universe from a sole source. It is not enough to mentally understand the mutual relationship of all parts of the universe with this source. Only when this teaching is so deeply ingrained into one's world outlook that everything is perceived through its grace does it become a guiding and ennobling factor directing one's behavior. And then one can both understand and feel that this world — with all its materiality and corporeality — is absolutely illusory and that its existence depends upon the will of the Creator, the only true and absolute existence. The will of God is such that, in this world, humanity in general and Jews in particular, having been given freedom of choice, fiercely struggle against their baser nature in the name of serving the Creator.

Gradually I realized what it was in Chabad that attracted me so. Chabad paradoxically unites a rational approach to reality with purely irrational belief, the most realistic pragmatism with the highest idealism. This combination does not at all impair the integrity and harmony of the world outlook and attitude which are so deeply characteristic of Chabad. Torah and life are not purposefully and consciously united and connected, but rather are interwoven and interfused into an organic unity. Every action, step and word of a Chabadnik emanates from his comprehension of God, the Torah, and the Rebbe and thus are derived from a single source. The exemplary Chabadnik of our generation, Ben-Zion Shem Tov, would say that our trouble is that we do not realize how good it is, how happy we ought to be that we have such a God, such a Rebbe, such wise and noble laws.

Of course this integral unity is refracted in different ways by different natures and sometimes is considerably distorted by personal idiosyncrasies. Therefore only outstanding personalities manifest this beauty and harmony. Yet if the distinctive and stable characteristics in the lives of most Chabadniks were to be isolated, this harmony would be clearly revealed.

29 At the end of 1966 signs of the Jewish exodus from the Soviet Union came to life. A few families received permission to get exit visas. True, most of them were elderly, but their departure evoked a new wave of excitement. We, however, still didn't have anyone in Israel to send us an invitation.

I visited all the emigrants before they left, sometimes even accompanying them as far as Moscow, plying them with requests which they probably forgot even before crossing the border. I also tried to clarify our chances of getting evicted to Rumania, as my father had been a Rumanian citizen. In 1941 the Soviet regime had given him a Nansen passport, making us in essence Soviet citizens through illegal means. But all these plans proved to be totally impracticable.

June 1967. The Six-Day War moved not only Jews but also Russians, who suddenly discovered that Jews know how to fight. The always hostile Latvians respected the Jews as allies resisting the Soviet regime. Many Jews who previously had known only vaguely about the existence of the State of Israel or who had cautiously put this subject aside, now began to speak about it and about their need to go and live there.

The number of young people attending the synagogue on holidays increased. True, they still mainly congregated in the courtyard. On Simchath Torah there was no end to the dancing and singing inside the building and on the street. The work on the graves of our brethren of the Riga ghetto at Rumbula was intensified, along with the gatherings there.

I would spend entire evenings by the radio, listening to all the Israeli broadcasts in succession — first in Russian, then in Yiddish, Hebrew and English — petrified that I would miss the most minute or seemingly trivial detail of this miracle of miracles which went down in history as the "Six-Day War."

Only one thing perplexed me. It seemed natural after such an obvious miracle for all Jews to immediately turn to God or at least to instinctively express some form of thankfulness to Him. Most of all I expected this from the Jews living in Israel. However, outside of a few exceptions, nothing like this happened. Moreover, Israeli statesmen stubbornly avoided using even the most natural expressions like "thank God" or "with God's help" which frequent the speeches of other leaders of other countries in the free world. I gathered the impression that most of our leaders then were pathologically protesting against God.

Skipping ahead, I might add that similar thoughts have continued to upset me every time that the Almighty performs a miracle for His people but is given neither acknowledgment nor gratitude. For example, in the beginning of the 1970's the bloodshed of the Arab terrorists trying to destroy Israel was turned against their fellow Arabs during "Black September" in Jordan. Despite the fact that it was impossible to explain this rationally by attributing it to the sophistication or strength of Jewish arms, again the miracle was not acknowledged and on the whole gratitude was not expressed.

I can't help but to contrast and compare such events with the passages from *parashath lech lecha*, where, after Abraham, our forefather of blessed memory, returns from a brilliant victory over Kedorla'omer and his allies, God suddenly says to him: "Fear not, Abram, I am a shield to you; your reward shall be very great." Rashi explains: Abraham feared that the victory which had been granted him exhausted the reward that he

deserved. This feeling of being indebted to God is catastrophically lacking in the present generation.

30 In early 1968 dozens of families finally
succeeded in getting permission to leave
Russia. This time there were actually young people among the
emigrants, as well as those with higher education and with
military obligations. Some Chassidic families also left. The
chances for *aliya* were demonstrably increasing. Notke took
heart, and he selflessly collected ancient Hebrew manuscripts
which could now be saved by being taken out of the Soviet
Union. He traveled throughout Russia, and my Sunday excursions with him became more infrequent but did not cease. Those
trips in my old, small car to Lithuania for chicken had become
almost a habit. We would leave before dawn and then pray and
breakfast somewhere in the forest after the sun rose.

These trips can show the relativity of the notion of everyday
hardships. Those of my relatives who knew about the trips
would say: "He's obsessed. To waste his entire day off, without
sleeping half the night, to be jolted about for three hundred
kilometers in a broken-down car just to haul back live, stinking
hens which have to be plucked after slaughtering — all this for
the sake of getting pieces of kosher meat for the family. This is
too much! Only a crazy fanatic can't understand that the Jewish
law allows for exceptions under such circumstances!"

But, honestly, not only was this not difficult but, on the
contrary, it gave me great pleasure. I was simply fulfilling that
which was required of me. In addition, Notke's Chassidic stories
about Yisrael Ba'al Shem Tov were especially inspiring when
told against the background of delightful rural landscapes.

A wonderful world was revealed in these stories. This
world — which by logical reasoning was so distant and strange to

me — awakened secret reminiscences through which it became precious and immediate. The purity of spirit and the nobility of the people living and acting in that world, their selflessness in helping their fellow Jew and in serving God, their constant gathering of "Divine sparks" cast into the lowest spheres of life, saturated this world with unique atmosphere and moods. The Holy One blessed be He clearly showed His presence in this world.

I will not conceal the fact that at first these stories, full of miracles and the supernatural, troubled the skeptical shell of my soul. I was inclined to understand them allegorically. It took some time until I reached an understanding of their simple literal meaning and until I realized that the bustling activity of our habitual world is illusory when compared with the world possessing the greatest degree of genuine existence, the world of the Ba'al Shem Tov.

31 In the spring of 1969, before Pesach, Notke and his family left also. After receiving the permit, he came home and started running around the room, extraordinarily excited, repeating over and over: "Fine fellow!" When his astonished household asked him who the fine fellow was, he replied, "The Almighty of course. He made them give us the permission to leave to go to *Eretz Hakodesh.*" Thus, here too, Notke remained true to himself, expressing his unbounded faith combined with an intimate rapport with Ha-Kadosh Baruch Hu.

Because I didn't know anything about the fate of my manuscript in Israel, Notke suggested that I give him a copy of it. It was a serious risk he took in spiriting the manuscript out of Russia. After arriving in Israel, he helped publish the book under his suggested title of *Mima'amakim (From the Depths)*, taken from the Psalms of King David.

Although I was lonely without Notke, I felt more confident knowing that my loyal friend was "over there." During that time I defended my doctoral dissertation. Shortly afterwards I was appointed a full professor. Some interesting invitations were sent to me from abroad. In particular I was invited for a university lecture tour in the United States. Not only was I not allowed to go, but I was instructed to reply that my wife was ill and I was not able to leave her. Incidentally, for a long time afterwards I continued to receive expressions of sympathy and wishes for my wife's recovery from my colleagues abroad.

I still didn't have a single concrete peg upon which to hang my request to leave the Soviet Union. I could not allow myself to embark upon a new fabrication after my Polish escapade with Rufina and Yusek and all my unpleasant experiences with the K.G.B. Moreover, I still didn't have any actual close relatives in Israel to invite me. Therefore I decided to wait a while, in agony that perhaps I was letting the last possibility escape.

I continued to work at the Academy, but it was increasingly difficult to concentrate on my work. My research seemed more and more meaningless and my colleagues and graduate students unbearably tiresome. These people were sincerely and firmly convinced that they were the pillars and motivating forces of human progress. The atmosphere at scientific conferences and conventions especially re-inforced this self-affirmation. These were actually celebrations of the greatness of the scientific elite — from the theatrical grandeur of the festive openings, to the refined pleasure experienced through demonstrating one's erudition and mental acuity during the discussions, to the strained wit of the banquet toasts while rubbing elbows with an eminent authority — and, above all, prevailed the sweet realization of self-aggrandizement along with the historical significance of the event. I write this not to judge others but to describe how I myself once had conceived my mission as a scientist, particularly at scientific conferences.

32 In the summer of 1968 the Soviet invasion into Czechoslovakia put an end to Dubcek's unprecedented experiment of creating "Communism with a human face." At that time I was concentrating entirely on Jewish problems and was little concerned with truth and justice on a global scale. Yet this invasion provoked an inexpressible feeling of disgust and resentment that unimpeded brute strength can destroy everything noble in this world.

Time passed, but there still was no hope, not even the smallest possibility, of leaving. Nevertheless I increasingly felt that the day was coming nearer when it would be possible to go. As I have mentioned earlier, on the surface hardly anything changed, but in truth everything was bound up in the exodus. Indeed, I continued to write articles and books on magneto-hydrodynamics, but it became more and more difficult to concentrate on these subjects. I gradually resumed my open participation in Jewish activities, attending the synagogue again instead of the secret *minyan*, and this gave me great pleasure. It didn't matter that the synagogue was located on the other side of town and that on Shabbath and holy days I had to walk four kilometers to get there and four kilometers back, in the heat of summer and the cold of winter, morning and evening.

I was especially moved by the month of Elul. This is the last month before the New Year — Rosh Hashana — designated for the Jews as a time of spiritual stock-taking and self-improvement. In the course of the last days of this month special prayers — *selichoth* — are read. They are recited in the early morning, long before the rising of the sun.

It was a wonderful sensation — rising in the middle of the night to walk to the synagogue through the dark, empty streets. The cold night would smell of the autumn dampness, of fallen leaves. I would pass groups of mushroom pickers with baskets and buckets, who were piling into trucks that were taking them from the city to the forests. And we few Jews would go forth with the knowledge that we were doing what our grandfathers and our great-great-grandfathers did at this time of the year — prepare for the days of Judgment and renewal and plead with our Creator to inscribe all our brothers from the four corners of the earth in the Book of Life.

We went to be judged before the Omniscient, and it was both awesome and joyous. Reciting and hearing the *selichoth* prayers evoked in me thousands of associations, reconstructing the atmosphere of *shtetl* life in the Jewish Pale of Settlement long, long ago. I could see and feel how the old *shammes*, huddling in a tattered *kapota* against the pre-dawn chill, would tread from house to house, knocking on closed shutters, reminding the Jews that it was time for the Almighty to bestow blessings upon His children scattered in a hostile, cold world. And the Jews would leave their dilapidated homes and hurry to the little wooden synagogue, dimly lit by flickering candles and kerosene lamps. Old men with beards and young boys with curling *pei'oth* — (sidelocks) . . .

I would be filled with nostalgia and longing for the *shtetl* — physically poor but spiritually overflowing with upward ascending spirit. These reminiscences were an inexhaustible source of moral admonition and inspiration during the whole year and especially on the eve of the Day of Judgment and Repentance.

There was always the feeling at this time of the year that we were heading toward something great, joyous, a little frightening, but most of all exalted. It was somewhat similar to how I used to feel before exams when I was a student, but now this was infinitely more important and elevated. And along with the awe and the inexpressible feeling of heightened expectation, pride and even a sort of gloating overcame me when I saw that the supposedly all-powerful Soviet regime — with all its army, uniformed and secret police, ubiquitous Communist Party, tanks, airplanes and atom bombs and gargantuan state machine — stood powerless to prevent a handful of unarmed defenseless Jews from serving their eternal God.

For the autumn holidays themselves I usually went to Transcarpathia. There vestiges of Jewish communities were still preserved. These communities were not as strong as those in Georgia, but in compensation most of their Jews were far more learned in Torah. Dozens of *minyanim* and *mikva'oth* were still functioning. During my visits there I became friends with yet another wonderful person — Yosef Mordechai Kagan, the underground rabbi for Mukachev and all Transcarpathia.

Officially Yosef Mordechai took in empty bottles at a glass collection station built in the courtyard of his house, but his real work was leading the Jewish life of Mukachev, Khust, Ujgorod and other towns. The life story of this man was horrible. His first wife and six children were killed in Auschwitz. Miraculously he survived and, thanks to his deep faith, was able to make himself return to live and work and even to build a new family. Then, from 1950 to 1953, to avoid arrest, he hid from Stalin's bloodhounds, sent out for his arrest. There were entire days and nights that he spent buried under mud in a ditch by the road, but never once during those three years did he forego a single *mitzva*. While this was going on, his second wife heroically raised four little children. When I knew him, his hair was entirely gray, even though he was well below sixty. Incidentally, he was the first Jew with *pei'oth* whom I had ever seen. He now lives in Brooklyn.

In the home of Rabbi Yosef Mordechai I learned a great deal about Jewish laws and customs. Among other things I acquired the art of baking fragrant Shabbath *challoth* and since then I have baked *challa* at our home for every Shabbath.

The time I spent in Transcarpathia was wonderful. Contact with Soviet reality was suspended, almost completely broken. Everything was devoted to God, Torah and the Jewish people *(am Yisrael)*; every minute was filled with Jewish learning.

During the Ten Days of Penitence between Rosh Hashana and Yom Kippur, I devoted many hours each day, in the Chassidic tradition, to reading *Tehillim*, the Psalms of King David. I recited the entire book up to three times a day, and once I was able to repeat the reading a full five times in the course of a single day.

Meanwhile our son, Geka, was growing up, and this created new problems. We had to protect him from the pernicious influences of the outside environment and open the wisdom and harmony of the Torah to him as early as possible, while taking care that he not give us away. By age one-and-a-half to two years he already knew quite thoroughly the difference between Shabbath and weekdays, between kosher and *treif* food. By age three he not only had mastered the Hebrew alphabet, but he knew many Hebrew words and could read a few simple ones. But at the same time he had to understand that not only were there Jews and non-Jews, but that only with "good Jews" could he talk about the prayers which he was starting to read from the *siddur*, about Shabbath and about Hakadosh Baruch Hu. He adjusted well to all the rules of the conspiracy. With only rare exceptions he knew how to determine by himself with whom he could speak about what. Naturally at home he wore a *yarmulke*, which he adroitly hid in his pocket whenever anyone came to us. And visitors came often because we were still living at the academic residences of Salaspils, so most of our neighbors were my colleagues. Neighbors were always coming to borrow kitchen utensils, to the point that we had to amass a special set of *treif* equipment for lending purposes. On Shabbath we had to light the candles behind the closet in a back room of our apartment. Often in the middle of our Shabbath meal uninvited visitors would show up. We would sit with them for hours in the front room, while the food that Fania had cooked got cold and dry. For the Pesach *seder* we would cover the windows with black curtains as if for an air raid. We would open the door only to those who knocked in a special way agreed upon in advance. Later we changed apartments, moving to the center of Riga to a house inhabited by people we didn't know, so this problem became less acute.

Geka loved hearing about Jewish history, about our forefather Abraham, about Moshe Rabbeinu and King David, about the Exodus from Egypt, about the Temple in Jerusalem. He presented many questions about the incorporeality of God, about the human soul and about the Holy Land of Israel which he longed for more than the most enticing toys. When he started going to school a new problem arose — how to free him from studies on Saturday. I still was not ready to sacrifice my work at the Academy, so I decided not to do as my friends the Chassidim did — either not to send Geka to school at all or to go to the principal and demand that our son be released from Saturday classes because we were religious. We chose the more cowardly path; we obtained a doctor's letter testifying that Geka's state of health necessitated his having two days of rest a week.

33 More and more Jews were leaving. The emigrants began to include non-religious people as well as those who had not belonged to the Zionist movement before the advent of the Soviet regime, and even those who had not been recently drawn to either Judaism or Zionism. These Jews, who seemed to be indifferent to everything Jewish, apparently were being carried along by the tide. A peculiar "chain reaction" was going on. The departure of one Jew "stimulated" others to go — relatives, neighbors, colleagues.

The most important advance in the exodus movement was the entry of Dr. Mendel Gordon into the battleground. This shy, quiet, young Rigan doctor was the first Soviet Jew with a PhD to get permission to leave for Israel. Mendel was the first to devise and test most of the tactics which later became the trademarks of the "refuseniks." He sent back his Soviet identification papers several times to Moscow and renounced his Soviet citizenship. This left him unemployed, homeless and hungry. Although Mendel came from a religious family in Dvinsk, he had long been far removed from Judaism. Now, having entered into single-handed combat against the Communist regime, he at once returned to the ethics of his fathers. It must be said that at that time — in the early 1970's — the search of young Jews, especially academics, for the way back to Torah was becoming a fairly widespread phenomenon in Riga, Leningrad and Moscow.

I was very interested in these people who were taking the same path that I had fortunately chosen earlier. This interest did not consist only of a feeling of special kinship, but of definite practical considerations as well. It was important for me to understand the motives driving these people to Judaism and Torah, so that this spontaneous process could be intensified and stimulated.

It turned out that the majority of them were not at all moved by recognizable philosophical reasons. Ethical-moral aspects held more importance for many. And there were many also who moreover found it difficult to analyze their reasons for turning to Torah. Sometimes negative factors played a major role: offense inflicted by a hostile environment, difficulties in getting accepted to a university or in advancing in work. But often there were positive factors contributing to the rekindling of their Jewish spark such as chance gleanings of information about the Torah and Jewish laws and customs. One person, for example, was stimulated by reading the last chapter in Deuteronomy, in which the Jewish people are warned about turning away from God and are told of the punishments and disasters that would befall them if they do. When he compared this with what was going on in the world, the realization of the total fulfillment of the prophecy made him shudder. This was the turning point of his life. Another one read *The Jewish War* by Feuchtwanger and started his return from there. There were many others who by chance (or so it seemed to them) met a Chabad Chassid and, through accepting an invitation to spend Shabbath with a religious family or even to put on phylacteries just once, they discovered a new world for themselves.

These people were all young. Most of them had a university education. Although differing in many ways, they were all equally wholehearted in their devotion to their newly discovered Torah, for which they were prepared to happily undergo any sacrifice or deprivation. Their new life-style presented numerous problems at work and in their studies. But possibly even more difficult for them were conflicts that arose with parents and wives.

It's questionable whether the Hebrew term for penitents — *ba'alei teshuva* (meaning literally "returnees") — is appropriate for people who had never even heard before of anything Jewish to which they could later return. At any rate, the life history of every one of them was a moving tale. I shall mention here only a few of the dozens of *ba'alei teshuva* whom I knew. For example, there was David Kajdan of Moscow University. One of the most talented mathematicians of our generation, he became an able student of *gemara* within a few years of learning almost entirely by himself. Or take Shmuel Raphaelson, a boy from Riga who became impassioned with Judaism at age twelve and spent months living on bread and water when he was unable to obtain kosher food. Or Tzvi Epstein, a teacher from Kolmna who would spend eight hours a day traveling to and from a remote school where he was allowed to teach without taking his hat off. The people mentioned here have left Russia, but hundreds of new *ba'alei teshuva* are constantly springing up in Riga, in Moscow, in Leningrad, in Tashkent.

After many ordeals, Mendel Gordon won and was given permission to leave. His success bore great psychological significance which strongly influenced others. It was apparent now that the situation of young Jews holding advanced academic degrees was no longer hopeless!

The Chassidim were leaving one after the other. As the

number of Chassidim in Riga declined, my personal responsibilities in helping to maintain Jewish life and education within the local community increased, as did my duties in writing and disseminating literature on Jewish and Israeli subjects. This demanded more of my time than my work at the Academy and limited my collaboration with *aliya* activists. My friends and I considered Jewish education to be even more important in the long run than *aliya* because any Jew who had even just an iota of Jewish education would soon be found in the ranks of those fighting to leave for Israel.

At that time, June 1970, the "National Co-ordinating Conference of Fighters for Jewish Emigration" took place. Sad to say, the politicking was so great that before the conference even opened, political quarrels had broken the assembly into factions, the number of which seemed to exceed the number of participants. This picture contrasted sharply with that of our Chassidic movement, where no one sought glory or rushed to express his opinions. Chabadniks preferred to concentrate on tedious mundane tasks with clear results and tremendous moral satisfaction.

And then, the famous Leningrad "Airplane Affair" occurred, followed by related court trials which agitated the entire Jewish world. On the one hand there was worry and concern for those who had been arrested, and on the other hand there was joy and pride that the *aliya* movement had become so strong. However, even in this stormy period charged with pro-Israel consciousness, the number of Jews actually affected by this awakening remained an extremely modest minority among the total three million Jews in the Soviet Union.

There were far more Jews who only passively sympathized with those of their brothers who were finding their way back. These passive sympathizers thirsted to know what was happening on the Jewish front, as these events aroused within them sweet memories of their childhood and of their parents' and grandparents' homes. However, they clearly rejected the possibility of participating in Jewish activism because, in the final analysis, they valued Russian culture, their professional careers and their orderly lives far more than these emotions and sentiments. There were other Jews in the Soviet Union who were openly hostile to the awakening Jewish movement, which they saw as a threat to their well-being. And finally, the vast silent majority of Soviet Jewry not only did not participate in these events, but—as unlikely as this may sound—they were hardly aware that anything was going on. All that interested these people were material matters such as a better, private apartment, a car, a dacha, exclusive imported clothes, enrolling their child in a university.

There is another group which could be mentioned here—the Jews who comprise the core of the "Democratic Movement," struggling to change the situation within Russia. The only thing they have in common with the *aliya* movement is a common enemy. This small movement enjoys neither mass support nor any chances of success. It sprang up, apparently, only thanks to the success of the Jewish *aliya* movement—the only movement during the entire Soviet regime to oppose government policy and to achieve its aims. (I doubt that anyone can provide a rational explanation for the success of the Jewish movement in Russia.)

The "Democratic Movement" presented a complication for the Jewish movement. However, the most immediate, dangerous enemy of the Jewish awakening was and still is Judeo-Christianity. The center of this movement is in a Moscow church, headed by an exceedingly enterprising convert (from Judaism to Christianity). Exploiting the fact that the Russian Jews who are now thirsting for spirituality are catastrophically ignorant of Judaism (the way back is blocked by many linguistic, cultural and psychological barriers), this Judeo-Christian leader and his cronies lure unwary souls by the easy accessibility of their poisoned wares. For some time this group has been obsessed by a large ambition. They want to establish their church in Israel.

Toward this end, they have been channeling people to Israel who are instructed to outwardly behave as Jews, even as believing, observant Jews. The tragedy is that for secular Jews both in Russia and in Israel it is very hard to sense the danger and the far-reaching consequences of this threat.

34 In the summer of 1971, the new developments finally reached us. My sister's and my brother's families left one after the other. A little later I received a *vizov* from them — a genuine, authentic invitation to come live in Israel. At last after so many years of waiting and wanting to leave, I was able to take positive action.

This did not mean that the express route to the Promised Land now lay open before me. This did not even mean that I could realistically expect that they would let us go in the near future. But it sufficed that I no longer had to sit idly by, shuddering at the thought that the door, opening ever so slightly to freedom, might be slammed shut at any moment.

During my long years under Soviet rule, I had collected papers, documents and photographs many times for all kinds of institutions, but never had I done this with as much enthusiasm as I did now. It didn't matter that Fania and I had lost our jobs. It didn't matter that I had absolutely no idea what we would live on while waiting to receive permission to leave. And this could take years.

The day that I brought the papers to the Department of Visas and Registration (O.V.I.R.) of the Ministry of Internal Affairs was one of the happiest days of my life. Outside of the fact that this was the first step on the way to Israel, I immediately felt freed from many chains that had been restraining me for years. I no longer had to worry about my job at the Academy. I no longer had to hunt for an "underground" *minyan* in a private apartment. No longer did I have to travel to Georgia or Transcarpathia for the High Holidays. I didn't have to hide my beret in my pocket anymore. I could even let my beard grow now, obeying the Jewish law not to "round off the side-growth of your head or destroy the side-growth of your beard."

It would not be an exaggeration to say that at the time I submitted my application for permission to receive a visa, I had reached the maximum success and prosperity possible in the Soviet Union. I was earning a top salary and had a flat in the center of town, a car and even a dacha on the shore of Riga bay. Moreover, I had achieved recognition as an authority in my scientific field of magnetohydrodynamics. I had published many articles, monographs and textbooks. I had students. If I had not "spoiled" my autobiography by my adventures with the Polish woman and the Israeli diplomats, then I surely would have been able to even travel abroad on business or to climb the administrative ladder.

According to any "normal" Soviet citizen, I had everything necessary for a quiet, orderly, fully satisfying and happy life. But this success only depressed me more, as it reminded me how far away I was from fulfilling my true aspirations. It was an achievement in the very opposite direction of that in which I wanted to go.

In distraction, I did everything possible so as not to feel this sweet prosperity. I deprived myself of needed sleep to spend hours poring over old Hebrew volumes which stubbornly would not yield to me. I would write and rewrite essays on Jewish-philosophical concerns. I wrote these essays only to burn them — either out of dissatisfaction with what I had written or out of lack of a place to keep them. I participated in all kinds of "illegal" Chassidic activities, free now to place my life in danger. And when and if I ever had a spare moment, I would sink into reverie about how someday I would help build the Land of Israel. Mostly I saw myself in the Negev desert seeking new ways to desalinate sea water. Sometimes my dreams linked my future with aeronautics (after all I was an expert in fluid dynamics!). I imagined myself spending sleepless weeks in Israeli laboratories working on endless experiments connected with development and defense projects.

It is no wonder, then, that when the long-awaited time came to take a stand for *aliya*, I happily rejected my worldly achievements — my security, my prestige and the opportunity to be scientifically creative.

About a month and a half after submitting our applications we received the expected refusal. I started to write endless letters and complaints. I made appointments with ministers and deputy ministers. I went to the Central Party Committee. The Latvian Minister of Internal Affairs told me that as I had worked in close contact under the same roof with people engaged in secret research, I couldn't help but know what they were doing, even though I never had "access" to secret work. Therefore, I would have to postpone my emigration until I forgot everything. "It's possible that they'll give you permission in five years," he said. "But then again, it might take ten to fifteen years."

I can't say that this encouraged me, but my morale was still much better than before I submitted my request. A number of Chassidim still remained in Riga, and they hastened to encourage me. Foremost among them was Shlomo Feigin. Studying Torah together with him became even more vital and joyful for me. I delighted also in being able to participate at the synagogue every day of the week, and I tried not to miss any of the public prayers.

It was wonderful to go to the synagogue openly, just as I would go to my own house. I have already written here that, to a great extent, ever since meeting the Chassidim I stopped feeling the authority of the Soviet regime, as from then on everything that happened in my life was on such a high spiritual plane that the K.G.B. was powerless to interfere. Having to pretend and lead a double life, keeping secret everything connected with observing the *mitzvoth*, had nonetheless been a terrible burden and constraint. Now I could walk proudly to the synagogue with nothing to hide.

How happy I was to get up just before daylight to ride or walk through the city, holding *tallith* and *tefillin* and talking with Jews about Torah and the Jewish destiny. On Shabbath after the morning prayers I would stay in the synagogue for *kiddush* and then sit for a long time, listening to explanations of the weekly *sidra* of the *Chumash* and endlessly enjoying the spiritual warmth and the atmosphere of brotherhood.

35

I continued to write complaints and to protest. Soon I started getting phone calls from abroad: from London, Paris, New York, Geneva and many other cities. The leaders of various movements for Soviet Jewry, students, women's groups, senators, and the chief rabbis of England, France and Israel phoned. Chief Rabbi Unterman's call from Israel especially excited me, of course. Several Nobel Prize winners and members of the Nobel Committee in Sweden also telephoned me saying that they were considering me as a nominee for my accomplishments in magnetohydrodynamics. Horrified by the idea that this could be an additional obstacle blocking my way to Israel, I begged them to leave me alone. Then again, Senator Walter Mondale called, asking me what I wished to say to the U.S. Senate.

Knowing the absolute indifference of the Soviets to public opinion, I could not see how this would help me. I would try to explain to the person at the other end of the line that I would prefer a statesman or scientist or writer on good terms with the Soviets to act on my behalf. My interlocutor was usually so intoxicated with his organizational success that he was too excited to listen to me patiently, so all I could do was to thank him cordially. All this ingratiation would take place at three o'clock in the morning, after I had already gotten up for several other calls — talking in English, no less — and knowing that the

K.G.B. was recording everything. I honestly admit that it was not very pleasant.

Eventually the K.G.B. cut off my phone. At that time I established contact with some of the Riga *aliya* activist groups, which were bitterly hostile to one another most of the time. I started to participate in their activities — collective letters, demonstrations, hunger strikes, mass marches to government institutions. Later I began to suggest ideas for various initiatives, a number of which were actually carried out. To tell the truth, however, this so-called struggle disgusted me. Its aim was not to bring any harm at all upon the regime that was tormenting us, but rather to simply attract attention to our demands. Moreover, this "struggle" had to be conducted very delicately so as not to cross over the fine line leading to prison.

I searched frantically for new forms of action which would truly hurt our enemies while, even more importantly, being good for us. Finally, I had it. Torah, collective study of Torah! What could be more dangerous to the Soviet powers than the study of Torah? And what could better guarantee the continuation and future of the *aliya* movement?! Not without reason had the Torah been one of the prime targets of the Communist regime ever since 1917. On the other hand, what could be more beneficial for us, preparing to settle in *Eretz Hakodesh,* than to become accustomed to Jewish learning?

I tried to explain to the *aliya* activists that for us, being unemployed and having so much spare time available in this interim period before our physical *aliya* provided a wonderful opportunity to regain the Judaism that our Soviet upbringing and education had denied us. Alas, it was very hard to make these people see the necessity of becoming Jews in the full sense of the word right there, in the Soviet exile.

I submitted a request to all kinds of high government offices to permit us to set up a study circle on Jewish religion at the Riga synagogue. I did not doubt that permission would not be granted and that the authorities would simply not respond. But it was important that my request be registered. This gave us a trump card against any possible accusation that our studies were implicated with anything anti-Soviet.

While futilely waiting a month for a reply from the government, we started to meet in small groups at private homes. Starting from *aleph*, we explained the meaning of the Jewish people and the Torah, pointing out that just as it is a disgrace for an intelligent Russian not to know who Shakespeare, Repin and Beethoven were, so is it even more a disgrace for an intelligent Jew not to know who Ezra and Nechemia, Hillel and Shammai, or Yehuda Halevy were.

I should mention perhaps that for some of my former colleagues and Jewish acquaintances, my transition to open belief and observance of *halacha* aroused slanderous talk. Following a chimeric logic, they accused me of pretension. Sometimes they tried to disrupt the studies I organized. And toward this end, alas, they stopped at nothing, not even seeking the help of the Soviet government. This is a sad story, and I would prefer not to discuss it.

Seeing how much time and strength the refuseniks were wasting, I tried to devise more and more ways to channel their energy into Jewish self-improvement through strengthening their Jewish consciousness. It seemed strange that these people, who were so decisively breaking away from their past in order to fulfill the important *mitzva* of *aliya* to Eretz Yisrael were disregarding the other 612 commandments as well as other Jewish responsibilities. It was painful to see that most of these people, persecuted and suffering, did not turn their thoughts to God, seeking His help and support. Only rare exceptions among them did what the grandfathers and great-grandfathers of all of them would not have failed to do.

I could not help but compare these people with my many Chassidic friends who had already managed to leave Russia and become acclimatized in Israel. I realized more and more clearly that the best thing for these rootless refuseniks was to start to learn how to be *Jews* while still in Russia. Otherwise, after having totally broken off from their past, they stood in danger of becoming catastrophically alienated when they did get to Israel. With their immediate goal of *aliya* achieved, what would they do without the opposition of the Soviet regime to spur their emotions?

I tried to use every opportunity possible to draw attention to the spiritual aspect of what was happening to us. Thus at a gathering at Rumbula on Lag b'Omer, I talked about the meaning of this holiday so unknown to Soviet Jews. I tried to explain that with all the greatness that Bar Kochba personified in physical military strength, in historical perspective Rabbi Akiva — who personified spiritual strength — proved to be far greater.

All these efforts were like drops in the ocean. But, nevertheless, I saw that there were some people — although few in number — upon whom my persuasions and explanations were beginning to seem effective. And this was enough to keep me from despair and to make me continue.

At this time the K.G.B. and the police began to harass us more and more. Trying to intimidate me, they even accused me of having killed a child in a hit-and-run accident. After endless interrogations, they apologized for the "mistake." However, we continued to live in unbearable tension. Each knock at the door could mean a new arrest; every call — another interrogation by the regular or secret police. There is no sense in dwelling on this in more detail because hundreds of Soviet Jews have endured similar and often worse ordeals, which have been widely publicized in the media.

The tension was mounting, and I was getting quite anxious. I kept my brother in Israel informed of my worsening situation, and he made a tour of Europe and America in order to organize support for me from American Jews, prominent scientists and so forth.

For the first time I was able to experience how much I had

gained psychologically by acquiring faith. Dozens of times it saved me from despair. After pouring out my soul in prayer or submerging myself in Torah study, I again became uplifted and certain of our ultimate success. Geka had even more faith and was more certain than I that we would soon leave. And the anxiety only made Fania stronger. But my poor long-suffering mother could not take it. The tension drained her strength and aged her terribly.

36 In August 1972 the Soviet government started to demand ransom as repayment for the cost of the higher education of Jews who wanted to leave the country. At first it was hard to clarify the exact price of each diploma, but it was evident that my various diplomas were going to cost me a lot. I estimated that they would total tens of thousands of rubles. Even if I were able to continue working as before, it would take at least five to ten years — without eating or drinking — to raise the sums that were being demanded. And here I had been unemployed for a year without earning anything. (We had been living all this time by selling clothes which we received in packages from world Jewry. In particular, Notke had entrusted us to the care of the New York organization "Ezras Achim," which sent us things easy and profitable to sell.)

This new obstacle of diploma ransoming, however, did not shake our unwavering belief that we would surely leave in the near future. True, there were days when it seemed hopeless. Sometimes after a routine visit to the K.G.B. it seemed that these ordeals would never end and that the next time they called me, I would have to stay with them.

One day I gathered my courage and went to the post office to call the Lubavitcher Rebbe in New York. Although convinced that they wouldn't connect me with New York, in less than ten minutes I was talking with the Rebbe' secretary. The Rebbe gave me his blessings and assured me that we would soon receive permission to leave.

The autumn holidays came and went — our last holidays in the Soviet Union. Immediately after Simchath Torah we got permission to leave. Only a week before they had dragged me to the K.G.B. and intimidated me, and now suddenly — they were letting us go. It was all so pitifully simple and prosaic. They called me to come in, informed me, and presented a bill for my diplomas. Throughout the many years that we had waited for this moment, it had always seemed to us that when it came, the earth would stand still, thunder would roll and lightning would flash. But nothing of the sort happened. A petty clerk simply called us to her office and told us that permission had been granted. And now, when I am writing these lines, it's even hard to remember any details outside of the fact that it was most prosaic, with no orchestras playing.

Recovering from the happy shock, we started to study the bill that had been presented to us. It came to more that thirty-one thousand rubles. This far exceeded any amount of money which I had ever held in my hands at one time.

Some people tried to convince us not to even try to raise the money. They said that we should wait and protest and so forth. Our telephone started working again at that point, and among our callers from abroad were those who advised us to "boycott" this so-called "tax-on-education." Their advise seemed absolutely absurd to me. If the Soviet government were burning with desire to expel all its Jews while also demanding payment of this "tax," then perhaps, just out of spite, a Soviet Jew might decide not to leave and to fight to abolish this ransom. But considering that Jews had to wait years in order to receive permission to leave Russia, then the advice to protest and refuse to leave was not only stupid but, in my opinion, destructive.

Moreover, it was clear to me, now that I had finally gotten hold of the cherished permission to go to Israel, that a contemptible thing like money could not stand in the way — even if I had to work to pay it off to the end of my days.

In the end, everything worked out simpler and faster than ever anticipated. Both in Riga and in Georgia, Jews with money were found who trusted me and were willing to lend us all that we needed. Within a few days I brought a very heavy bundle to the bank. All the members of my family together with Bubi Tzeitlin (who came especially for this occasion out of his love for the extraordinary) could not count the piles of bank notes. None of us were experienced enough in money-counting.

From then on, everything went smoothly and happily. Running around to countless bureaucrats and waiting in long lines didn't bother me. It was even fun solving bureaucratic puzzles, for instance when office A doesn't give out form X until receiving form Y, given out by office B, but office B demands that it be given form X first, and so forth.

It took quite a lot of time to arrange for permission to transport my library. They made me pay the value of all my old books, even though they were my own. Furthermore, my entire collection (especially my old Hebrew volumes) had to be subjected to a thorough inspection, including leafing through pages and shaking bindings.

Yet, after two weeks we were sitting on board a train headed for the town of Brest on the Polish border. Many people had accompanied us to the railroad station. The door to our apartment had not been closed for twenty-four hours straight the day before we left. Relatives, friends, and even people we didn't know came to say good-bye. Many of them had requests or favors to ask which I either listed in my notebook, codified in secret code, or tried to commit to memory.

I had bidden farewell to the synagogue on my last Shabbath in Riga. *Kiddush* that day took several hours. The congregants parted from me with a heartfelt warmth which I shall never forget: trembling palms gripped in warm embrace; eyes pouring out benevolence and yearning, joy and hope and everlasting sorrow. The usual Shabbath singing, which somehow always sounded new, this time contained a special prayer, *Hoshia es amecha* ... ("Save Thy people and bless Thy heritage ..." — not just simply an abstract "save" but "save *us*, O ever-present and near God, our Protector, our own.") The beseeching words and melody soared upward to reverberate off the vaulted ceiling. Outside, all around, bustled the noise and exhaust fumes of the Soviet street. There, inside, under the arches of the cellar that housed the Chassidic synagogue, Shabbath tranquility reigned over Jews who, with overflowing hearts, were drinking *l'chayim* to their brother on his way to the Promised Land and wishing each other a speedy departure on the same path.

37 Thus, the train made its way to Brest, getting closer and closer to the border that I had so often envisioned and dreamed about. Before crossing the border, we still had one final confrontation with the Soviet regime — a baggage check. Before leaving Riga, I had burned most of my published and all unpublished manuscripts, notes and card files, so as not to waste time on making arrangements for mere papers in light of the more important and joyful occasion of our *aliya* to *Eretz Hakodesh*. So we thought that we held nothing seditious in our bags. It goes without saying that we also had neither gold nor diamonds on us. Nevertheless, they found forbidden objects in the search: bundles of old letters dear to me and a box of family movies and tapes. They ordered all this to be returned to the Soviet Union by our relatives who were accompanying us to the border.

Finally, we were back on the train. Ever so slowly, it moved toward the border. We were exhausted from the prolonged excitement, and so the longed-for moment of our dreams slipped by drably.

And then we were in Poland. In Warsaw the train stopped for more than an hour at a suburban platform. I was eager to finally step on non-Soviet soil. Moreover this was the Poland which I had unsuccessfully tried to reach fifteen years before. Taking Geka, I walked out onto the dark platform. We walked around a station warehouse. Everything within me was singing and rejoicing, but my thoughts were racing forward to that still distant, but now attainable, Mediterranean shore.

The next day we arrived in Vienna. There we were taken beyond the city to the Schönau Castle, where the Jewish Agency ran a transit camp for Russian Jews. We were accompanied there by Austrian policemen, armed with automatic rifles to protect us against Arab terrorists. Entering the castle, we heard people speaking Hebrew and saw large photographs of Israeli landscapes hanging on the walls. And we were choked with tears. An incomparable feeling of being among our own, among brothers, filled us with indescribable happiness.

We stayed at Schönau for a day and a half. There were group singing and song-teaching, lectures, films. There were Hebrew and Russian language books, journals and newspapers printed in Israel. It was an unpleasant surprise to see how mediocre and grammatically incorrect the Israel Russian-language publications were. But I had neither the time nor the inclination then to worry about such things. The holiday feeling at meeting my homeland prevailed over everything. And it was only just beginning.

The Jewish Agency workers — those indefatigable angels — put us aboard an El Al plane. We departed from Vienna after midnight, but I kept my eyes glued to the portholes, straining to discern something in the heavy darkness beyond. At last the Israeli coastline appeared beneath us. The lights of Tel Aviv shot through the darkness, and in a few minutes the plane was rushing along the runway. I would have liked to go back and relive those minutes, like going over slow-motion film, lingering upon and savoring every detail.

38 But it was already time to alight. Dawn was beginning to brighten the eastern sky. We stepped outside onto the stair-platform. The warm humid air of the Mediterranean night blew in my face. I looked down and stopped. Anxiety and confusion seized me. Twenty steps below me lay the Land of Israel—the land eternally promised to Abraham, Isaac and Jacob; the land to which Moses led the Jews; the land upon which had stood the First and Second Temples; the land to which generation after generation had turned in prayer and tears. Was I ready to meet this land? Did I have the moral right to tread on it, to soil it with my coarse shoes? Someone pushed me in irritation. I was blocking all movement out of the plane. I had no choice but to go down. Reaching the bottom of the stairs, I fell on my knees, bent over and kissed the ground. But, sensing the astonished stares of the passengers around me, I immediately got up.

Everyone was in a frightful hurry. Upon entering the airport building, they rushed to the tables where representatives of the Ministry of Absorption sat. Everyone was afraid of missing out on the best housing offers.

I was still trying to comprehend the magnitude of the occasion. Therefore, being reminded about mundane arrangements seemed to me to be disgraceful and blasphemous. Circumstances did not allow me, however, to concentrate on my thoughts. Not only my brother and Notke had come to meet me, but also Knesset member Avraham Verdiger (of the Poalei Agudat Yisrael religious party) and a number of newspaper and radio correspondents. Avraham Verdiger was the first person with whom I spoke in Israel. My throat was so parched from the excitement that I could not talk. Verdiger brought me some juice to drink, and gradually my voice returned.

Leaving the airport building I was met by a large group of Chabadniks from Riga and elsewhere, a representative of the religious university of Bar Ilan, and several people whom I didn't know. After kissing and embracing, the Chabadniks immediately broke into Chassidic dancing on the sidewalk, and we sang and danced for a long time. Then all my family got together at my sister's house in Rishon Letzion. It was Friday, Cheshvan 19, 5733. Before evening set in, we went to Notke's house at Lod to spend the first Shabbath in *Eretz Hakodesh* with him.

Exhaustion and a torrent of impressions and feelings of unimaginable enormity slightly subdued my euphoria. But, just the same, it was a holiday—an endless and unending holiday where human warmth, friendliness and benevolence prevailed. Dancing Chabadniks carried my son and me into the old synagogue in the Chabad section of Lod, overflowing with friends and acquaintances from Russia and with strangers, apparently people from the streets who recognized us from the photos and write-ups about our arrival in the newspapers. These people were all so genuinely happy about our *aliya;* they so sincerely wanted to help us and smiled in such a kind way.

39 Within a very short time I began to be literally torn to pieces by invitations to every possible kind of meeting, soirée, and discussion. I had to learn how not to quail before large, strange audiences and to address them in Hebrew, English or Yiddish. I had never formally studied either Hebrew or Yiddish, except for one year of Hebrew in elementary school and a brief effort at independent study during my student years in Leningrad. However, learning Torah and the prayers with the Chabadniks in Riga had given me—among other things—the gift of two Jewish languages. It turned out that I could express myself in both of them quite adequately.

Two types of audiences intimidated me — religious Jews and children. The former intimidated me because of their immeasurable superiority in Torah. How could I — trying to compensate for what I had missed in my childhood — measure up to people who from early childhood on had systematically studied in *yeshivoth?* I remember how difficult it was for me to speak when they brought me for the first time to Kfar Chabad for a national conference of Lubavitch Chassidim in Israel. They wanted to hear about Jewish life in Russia. I stood in front of the microphone, looking at the enormous hall filled with gray-bearded Jews in black frock-coats. Alongside tremendous joy, fear overcame me. Who was I to appear before such people steeped in Torah wisdom? Finally, I got hold of myself and began to speak. Seeing hundreds of smiles and eyes radiating friendship, I calmed down.

I was always afraid to address an audience of children. Being aware of the tremendous responsibility involved, I would fear that I would not succeed in convincing them or in establishing genuine contact.

Among my impressions of that time, I remember my first visit to Jerusalem. Avraham Verdiger invited Fania, Geka and me to the Knesset. All four of us went there, together with my brother and his wife. On the way from Tel Aviv, I was afraid of missing the smallest detail of the landscape. After the littered eyesores and rusted wrecked car dumps of the outskirts of Tel Aviv, there followed cultivated fields and kitchen-gardens, irrigated by water sprayers, and tidy little houses of agricultural settlements. Finally the eucalyptus tree-lined road brought us to the Valley of Ayalon. At the other end of the valley, the Judean hills floated in the haze. Ten minutes later we were already traveling through these hills.

My excitement was growing by the minute. It seemed that we were approaching far too fast, at a pace that did not allow me to collect my thoughts and prepare myself spiritually to meet the Holy City. And indeed Jerusalem caught me by surprise. The disinterested car engine sped us uphill at eighty kilometers per hour, and suddenly I found myself in Jerusalem. I did not notice then the unique Jerusalem sunlight, multiplied by the reflection of the golden Jerusalem stone. I did not notice the quaint, alluring side streets climbing up the hill slopes. I was distressed that here I was, standing in Jerusalem, *Ir Hakodesh*, but I had not yet managed to prepare anything to offer. Tears of happiness and gratitude welled in my eyes.

On that first visit to Jerusalem, my chief worry was to make sure that I wouldn't find myself by chance at the Western Wall. This meeting demanded more thorough preparation. Only days later — on Rosh Chodesh Kislev — did I finally resolve to go to the Wall.

At first I kept count of my visits to Jerusalem, as each one was an event in itself. I counted up to twelve and then lost track. However, for a long time I was unable to get used to the fact that it was possible to say simply, "I'm going to Jerusalem" — and actually do it.

After a few months we went to America to see the Rebbe. I also had to give the seminars in several universities which had been postponed for so many years. I wasn't earning a living yet, but Chabadnik friends lent me the money for the trip.

Since leaving the Soviet Union, I have met and talked with many famous people — with presidents and prime ministers, distinguished scientists, writers and numerous Jewish and non-Jewish leaders and public figures. Many interesting things could be written about every one of these meetings. And if God grants me the strength and the opportunity, I'll do this — another time. Here, however, I want to describe only my most important and impressive meeting — with the Lubavitcher Rebbe, the great man and the great Jew and mentor of our generation.

40 I had been preparing myself and dreaming about this meeting for a long time. In every possible way I had tried to imagine what it would be like. I had heard a very great deal about this great man from Chassidim who had met him and were infinitely dedicated to him. I cannot deny that the degree of devotion, admiration and adoration for the Lubavitcher Rebbe sometimes bothered me. Although by then I was already quite steeped in the ideas of Chabad, this particular aspect of it disturbed me. It awakened echoes of scepticism which I had long since overcome. Therefore, I waited for my first meeting with the Rebbe with excitement and impatience, mixed with fear of disappointment.

I prepared myself for a personal reception with the Rebbe (*yechiduth*) just as a Chassid ought to prepare for a meeting with his spiritual teacher, *tzaddik* and intermediary between himself and God. I fasted the whole day before our meeting, cleansed myself in the *mikveh,* and girded myself in a *gartel* (prayer belt).

Several days before our private meeting with the Rebbe, we had attended our first *hithva'aduth* (a large gathering of Chassidim devoted to a significant date, a holiday, a Rosh Chodesh, or so on). Thus, I already knew how the Rebbe addresses thousands of Chassidim, *yeshiva* students and guests, unlike anything which I had ever seen before. The Rebbe spoke for five hours straight, not using any notes, *sichoth* and *ma'amarim* following one another in brilliant continuum.

Skipping ahead, I want to mention that often the Rebbe devotes his discussions to an analysis of a commentary of Rashi on the *Chumash*. In these commentaries — which for centuries every Jewish boy learned — the Rebbe finds completely new aspects, undiscovered depths, and unnoticed revelations. He shows how incomprehensibly capacious is this terse commentary, how the position and weight of every letter and word is so precise and intended, and yet how many passages sound topical and applicable to modern Jewish life. The proof of a conclusion can last one or two hours — sometimes more. The Rebbe scrupulously analyzes and compares details, prepares an attack on the problem from various sides, and with a jeweller's precision threads the intermediate secondary results onto the core of the evidence. He dwells for a while on one line of thought, leaves it for another, to return to the first. And suddenly the final conclusion is reached: clear, brilliant, irrefutable and ... unexpected.

The unshakable logic; the ultimate scholarliness and systemization of the explanations and proofs; the perfect accuracy of the references to pertinent passages from the oceans of Talmudic and Chassidic literature quoted by heart; the inaccessible heights of Kabbalistic abstractions; and the touching simplicity of examples and comparisons taken from life — this is but a pale reflection of the impression made by the Rebbe's speech. And all this is radiated with such love for the Jews, the Torah, and the Almighty and is inspired by such deep emotions that your heart becomes warm and glad and your first thought after many hours of listening is: "When will I have the good fortune of hearing the Rebbe again?"

During the brief intermissions of the speech, the entire audience unites into a many-thousand-voiced choir, singing Chassidic melodies. The Rebbe exchanges *l'chayim* with hundreds of participants. The atmosphere is always very solemn and ennobling, yet at the same time unbelievably intimate and earthy. You feel as if you were at the *beith hamikdash* itself, yet the warmth and ease reminds you more of your father's home. What is most elating to see and difficult to comprehend is that in this day and age several thousand people happily come to listen to the most profound teaching and stay for a number of hours, many of them standing, keeping prolonged absolute silence. And what overwhelming enthusiasm rallies these thousands of souls into one body! Nowhere else in the world can you see such a phenomenon!

Our private reception with the Rebbe took place after midnight. The Rebbe had already held about fifty such private meetings that night. Yet, his face showed no signs of fatigue. From the moment we entered his office, Fania, Geka and I felt as if we had known him for many years and were continuing a conversation begun long ago. The Rebbe gave us attention and interest such as we had never felt before, not even from our closest relatives. I was astonished how well informed the Rebbe was about politics, about various natural sciences, literature, economics, and the situation in Israel and in Russia. His greatness in Torah is well known, and therefore goes without saying. Most incredible was how much the Rebbe knew and remembered about our personal and family affairs and circumstances.

And finally — his wonderful eyes. Sky-blue and pure, sometimes they penetrate through and through, making the interlocutor actually feel the omnipresence of his attention and involvement. And sometimes they sparkle with a thousand smiles. Between these extreme expressions are countless others which never seem to be repeated but are all alike in their infinite dedication to the person with whom he is talking.

My fear of being disappointed vanished immediately and completely. I later met the Rebbe many more times and spent many hours listening to him speak about the eternal problems of the Jews, about events of the day, difficult philosophical problems or about the daily concerns of governments and individuals.

I am amazed every time the Rebbe reminds me of the contents of a previous discussion, held one, two or three years before. Often it happens that I have completely forgotten even the subject or event, but the Rebbe reminds me of the most minute details. I have already mentioned that in the past years I have met many famous people — politicians, scholars and writers. But I have never met anybody who can listen like the Rebbe can, who not only is a concerned listener but who cuts off all other disturbances and distracting interests. When speaking with other people, one always feels that most of their attention is engrossed in what happened before the conversation or in what is going to happen after it, or that they are simply preoccupied with their own concerns. When you talk with national leaders or world famous intellectuals, the clear majority of them in general are able to understand you only if you talk to them from a position geared to their own psychology. If you analyze a problem from a position unknown or unacceptable to them, they simply turn you off, like switching a radio to another station. Moreover, it always feels that they weigh their words only from the point of view of personal or party interests, or of their own prestige. And when it comes to giving advice or making a decision, they always try to avoid answering or to procrastinate. With the Rebbe, everything is completely different. No matter what you say or from what position or point of view you say it — all you have to do is to utter half a word — the Rebbe understands everything. The Rebbe is totally there with you when he talks with you and makes a decision or gives advice immediately. He does not have to confer with anyone. Nor does he weigh profits and losses. He just speaks the truth — absolute and unaffected. It is impossible to imagine him having "personal interests." And you always feel that his advice or decision is made only for the good of the Jews in general and of yourself in particular — both in the spiritual and in the simple, worldly sense.

Every time that I have the occasion to see how the Rebbe instantaneously makes a decision, I cannot help but to contrast him with other people whom I have seen when they were required to decide something. On the one hand, I recall the countless Soviet functionaries who pass the matter on to their superiors, and, on the other hand, I compare him with Israeli politicians whose resolution usually suffices, in a complex situation, to immediately establish another committee which, perhaps, will investigate.

The advice of the Rebbe is sometimes hard to accept. Sometimes it even seems illogical at first. But it is useless to try to break your head trying to figure out its rational basis. If you have the integrity and strength of will to follow the advice, without having found its rational basis, then you invariably will become convinced — sometimes months or years later — how infinitely right the advice was. And you also invariably will see where disregarding the advice would have brought you.

What gives the Rebbe this wonderful strength of foresight? A phenomenal memory and analytical mind? Continual study of Torah and the lack of personal, worldly aspirations (these last being two attributes which define the Jewish concept of a *tzaddik,* a holy man)? Or is there an unknown Divine revelation at work? Possibly, the infinite faith of so many Chassidim sets the Rebbe apart as the spiritual intermediary between God and man? I shall not try to answer. Perhaps the answer is all of these factors together. But it is certainly something far greater than the most exceptional human talents. Whatever it may be, the Rebbe is undoubtedly the only person in the world in whom I would unhesitatingly entrust the fate of my loved ones and my own self.

Oh, if only our long-suffering state had a leader possessing such love and concern for people, such strength of foresight, such decisiveness and such total lack of self-interest and personal considerations!

It is amazing that when talking with the Rebbe, you never feel overpowered by his superiority, by his great personality. The Rebbe is master of oceans of Torah and their innermost depths, whereas his interlocutor in most cases is only a beginning student in Torah. The Rebbe knows and remembers all the problems of the person with whom he is talking better than the person himself and is thus capable of giving the best possible advice and counsel. But the main thing is that the Rebbe perpetually devotes all his strength and all his time to Jewish affairs. He has no time off, no vacations, no so-called personal interests. His interlocutor, at best, sacrifices a part of his time and his livelihood for the greater good of the Jewish people, but his major involvement remains his career, his family, his success, amusement and relaxation. And despite this enormous disparity, the interlocutor is not necessarily aware of it and always feels at ease and unrestrained with the Rebbe.

The Rebbe displays deep respect for specialists of all fields. However, I know of dozens of cases — told to me by participants in the events — where the Rebbe expressed an opinion or gave advice contrary to that of specialists in politics, medicine, pedagogy or other fields, and in the end he was always proved to be right and the others wrong.

More than once, the Rebbe has given advice to Israeli statesmen on vital questions. It is most unfortunate that for the most part, either because of previous misconceptions or because of party discipline, Israeli politicians have not heeded the Rebbe's advice. I personally was present at a *hithva'aduth* a few days before the Yom Kippur War started. I heard the Rebbe warn us of the approach of this war and explain how Israel should react. Alas, even at that terrible hour his advice was not taken.

Many times I have heard the Rebbe discuss science, problems of establishing a unified world outlook based on the Torah and the meaning and interpretation of new developments in the natural sciences in light of this world outlook. The Rebbe can prove always the absurdity of trying to use science to "correct" the Torah. However, he does not repudiate science. He simply insists that science, like everything else which God created in this world, must serve the Jew in his quest for holiness and wholeness, for unity with God and Torah.

You can meet Jews from five continents at the Rebbe's reception room — rabbis and merchants, artisans and businessmen, writers and politicians, professors and government ministers. And every day sacks of letters are delivered, bearing thousands of requests for advice and guidance.

There is so much that could be said about the headquarters and world center of the Chabad movement at 770 Eastern

Parkway in Brooklyn. Hundreds of people from all corners of the earth, thousands of Chassidim living in the surrounding neighborhoods, *yeshiva* students and *ba'alei teshuva* pray in the large and small prayer halls, the corridors and stairwells. The ebullience does not subside here day or night. There is constant Torah learning, praying, discussion, singing.

What seems to the newcomer to be turmoil and disorder is known by the more experienced visitor to conceal the precise rhythm of life activity. Most importantly, one soon begins to feel the unique atmosphere of ennoblement, of holiness (but in no way hypocritical sanctimoniousness), of distinct separation (but in no way monasticism) which reigns here. Possibly, the Temple in ancient Jerusalem was like this. And, just as the pilgrims, coming from all corners of Eretz Yisrael to Jerusalem, brought back home inspiration and ennobled spirit, so do the visitors to "Seven-Seventy" (as the Chassidim call it) return home with a resolve to henceforth selflessly serve Hashem.

One of the true miracles of our age of Jewish renewal is the world-wide network of Chabad educational systems, founded by and ever constantly strengthened and further developed by the Rebbe. Schools, *yeshivoth*, Chabad Houses, Chabad representatives in university towns — these are the present outposts and bastions in the war against assimilation and for the return of Jews to the faith of their fathers. These fortresses are scattered throughout the globe, nearly everywhere that Jews are living: in Israel, in Australia, in London, in Miami Beach, in Johannesburg and in Milan, in Paris and in Philadelphia ... In some places, the staff of these institutions is quite large, and in others — a sole representative fearlessly mans his post alone, on behalf of the Rebbe, in the name of the Jewish faith and the future of Jewish children. These selfless people, who are for the most part graduates of Lubavitch *yeshiva*, without any secular education, move about in the thick of society, knowing everybody and everything, conversant in politics, philosophy, literature and business (in addition to, of course, their knowledge of Torah).

With the same ease they can carry out a living-room conversation, deliver a lecture on Jewish philosophy, or conduct a Talmud lesson. Heroically, they bear the burden of the enormous expenses needed to build and maintain the institutions which they are establishing. Up to their necks in debt, they sometimes are forced to spend a great deal of their time raising money from all kinds of businessmen. However, they never beg, they never lose their dignity, facing people with less Torah learning and mien than they.

Through these envoys, as through all his Chassidim, the Rebbe creates order and harmony in the Jewish world, which is prey to thousands of alien influences and prone to chaos and degeneration. To borrow an analogy from physics, the Rebbe changes the natural course of events by miraculously reducing entropy. The Rebbe's envoys—each one of whom is an outstanding personality who has confined his personal ambition to the service of an ideal—deserve our respect and admiration. Perhaps their families deserve even more praise, for they know neither vacations, days off, family seclusion, or simply a moment to catch their breath. May the Almighty send you health and strength, my new but faithful friends: Yitzchok Groner, Avramel Shem-Tov, the Lipskar brothers, Faivush Fogel, Nosan Gurari, Moshe Feller, and many, many others.

I must also mention my young friend who is still gleaning experience but whose devotion and self-sacrifice is beyond measure: Hershel Okunev. He is the director of F.R.E.E., a New York Chabad organization that provides Jewish education and many other kinds of help for Jews coming from Russia to America. Another outstanding individual is Shlomo Maidinchick, Council Chairman of the Israeli Chabad settlement, Kfar Chabad. A locomotive driver, he is friends with nearly all the generals of the Israeli army and enjoys free access to the President's house as well as to the Ministry of Defense. And how could I not mention Tzvi Greenwald? A former freedom fighter in the Lehi underground, he is now a teacher and probably the best Chabad orator in Israel. And, finally, there is so much that should be said about the Rebbe's dedicated secretaries and aides: Benyamin Klein, Laibl Groner, Yudel Krinsky, and of course Rabbi Chodakov, the Director of Chabad Headquarters.

Since the Six-Day War the Rebbe has been engendering a world-wide campaign to encourage Jews to fulfill some of the most important *mitzvoth*: putting on *tefillin*, having a kosher *mezuza* on every Jewish door, lighting Shabbath candles, teaching children Torah, and universally observing the laws of *kashruth*, family purity and so on. And now, in this ambiguous and anxiety-ridden time for our people, when the whole world is against us, thousands upon thousands of Jews in all corners of the world have been picking up little sparks of the Jewish soul and the Jewish way of life, thanks to the determined efforts of the Rebbe and his Chassidim.

And if we look at all this from the point of view of the interrelationship of all Jews with the Almighty — Who constantly creates anew all matter and life and elevates our world in proportion to the vitality and degree of holiness which we, His creations, attain here on earth — then it is very easy to understand why the Rebbe closes nearly all his *sichoth* on Jewish education and *mitzva* campaigns by mentioning the *Mashiach Tzidkeinu*. May our actions and thoughts prove worthy of bringing him forth speedily in our days.

41   Our so-called absorption into Israel was unusually smooth and happy. While still at Lod airport I received an invitation to work at Bar-Ilan University. A little later, the universities of Tel Aviv and Beersheva invited me, as did the Technion in Haifa. As I didn't have to spend time learning Hebrew first, the question of work had to be decided immediately. It was hard to choose. Beersheva especially attracted me because its university was very young and rapidly developing and because life in the Negev, in the heart of the desert, held a slight sense of pioneering. But even more than that, the ancient-modern town of Beersheva was deeply associated in my mind with Avraham Avinu, with his years in the Negev desert. However, as heavy pressure was being exerted by Tel Aviv University, I decided to combine working at both places.

And indeed, for more than a year I was full professor at both the Tel Aviv and Beersheva universities. A little later, the U.S. Department of the Navy signed a contract with me for research work in magnetohydrodynamics, and I had to decide where to build my laboratory. Although until then we had been intending to settle in Jerusalem, where I spend much time involved with my public work (which I shall describe later), in the end I chose Beersheva and we moved there.

How I got the U.S. Navy contract, how the Rebbe "engineered" me into it, is an interesting story.

As I have already said, my first visit to the Rebbe was part of a four-week trip to America scheduled shortly after I arrived to settle in Israel. A number of professional colleagues throughout America had also invited me to come visit their laboratories and lecture on my work. I was planning on resuming my teaching and research career (interrupted by my departure from the Soviet Union) as soon as I returned to Israel.

Near the end of my four-week stay in the U.S.A., a well-known Chabad activist, Rabbi Avraham Shem-Tov, invited me to come to Philadelphia to talk with Jewish students there. Before traveling to Philadelphia, I was received again by the Rebbe. Among other things, I mentioned this upcoming trip. The Rebbe was very interested in the details of my schedule in Philadelphia and afterwards added, as if incidentally, "When you're in Philadelphia, don't forget to meet with the scientist in your field at the university." This astounded me. I knew the names of all the American scientists working in magnetohydrodynamics of liquid metals as well as the universities where they worked, and I was absolutely certain that there was no one in Philadelphia of significant professional interest to me.

After greeting me at the Philadelphia railway station, Avraham Shem-Tov asked me what the Rebbe had talked about with me in *yechiduth*. Among other things I told him about the Rebbe's incomprehensible instruction to see a professional colleague in Philadelphia. "Apparently it's a misunderstanding."

"With the Rebbe there are no misunderstandings," imparted Shem-Tov. "Let's go straight to Temple University and the University of Pennsylvania and find this person."

I was bewildered. How could we look for him? And why go searching when I knew for certain that there was no laboratory, there was no specialist in my field at any university in that town. But it was impossible to withstand Shem-Tov's pressure. We went from building to building, from department to department, for many hours. We questioned dozens of strangers. They were surprised by our personal appearance and even more so by the questions we asked. And then, just before sunset, when the University of Pennsylvania was emptying out, someone in a dark corridor scratched his forehead and said, "Magnetohydrodynamics?...Just a minute...Professor Hsuan Yeh must be connected with that."

He explained how to find Professor Yeh, and in a few minutes we were sitting in his office. It turned out that Yeh, Chinese in origin, had been working many years in America on a number of magnetohydrodynamics projects conducted outside the auspices of the university. We spent several hours together. He described some of his findings but was even more interested in mine. On parting, he said, "The American Symposium on Magnetohydrodynamics is being held in five weeks, at Stanford. You must come and deliver a lecture. It's way past the deadline for submitting lectures, but I'm a member of the organizing committee and can arrange it, especially considering that you've just come from the Soviet Union."

I thanked him but refused, as I had to return to Israel that week.

Back in New York, I wrote the Rebbe a note about everything that had happened in Philadelphia, mentioning also Professor Yeh. The Rebbe answered immediately that the invitation to Stanford was of major importance and that I had to do everything possible to attend the conference. I didn't understand at all why this conference warranted ruining all my plans of starting work at Beersheva. But by then there was one thing I had learned: the advice of the Rebbe must be followed without argument, whether it makes sense to me or not.

Five weeks later I was at Stanford University in California. An hour after my arrival, even before I delivered my lecture, two representatives from the U.S. Office of Naval Research introduced themselves to me. They told me that they were well acquainted with my name and my work and that they wanted to offer me the opportunity to continue my research on magneto-hydrodynamic turbulence in liquid metals under contract with the American Navy. They understood that I intended to work in Israel and were prepared to finance my work there.

Since then, this agreement has been renewed six times already and has lasted six full years. During these six years I have set up and equipped my laboratory where I have managed to develop a new way of converting solar energy into electrical energy, which has become the chief focus of my work. This would not have happened in this way had not the Rebbe given me his strange, incomprehensible advice . . . not unlike a mysterious instruction of the Ba'al Shem Tov sending a Chassid to a remote village, telling him only that he must go visit the home of the local water carrier . . .

42 And so we settled in Beersheva. Fania began to work as a doctor at the local hospital, and Geka went to a *yeshiva* in Beersheva. Since early childhood he had been so imbued with thoughts about Israel that his transplantation to Israeli soil was a natural process, part of a continuum. As for myself, it seemed that after a forced interruption I was returning to my normal place. I felt linked with this land through all the past generations and through the Torah, far more than many Israelis whose only link to it is the circumstance of their birth here. I have never regretted choosing Beersheva in the Negev. On the contrary, only here am I able to understand and to see how my homeland is being built and beautified from day to day and to take my small part in it.

Only my poor mother couldn't adjust to our new living conditions. I had dreamed that Israel would bring her the happiness and satisfaction which she so much deserved after all her suffering. But, alas, she was almost seventy-five years old when she arrived. Learning Hebrew seemed impossible to her. All the familiar things to which she was accustomed had been left far behind. And she, poor woman, became very, very weak.

Right away I was faced with an old dilemma. Should I take advantage of the opportunity to enjoy a quiet, settled, orderly life or should I seek something greater? Indeed, I could conscientiously work at the university, teaching and doing research, publishing articles and books. And with all this, I would still have many hours for relaxation, reading, contemplating the spurs of the Judean hills seen from our window, or even cultivating roses or a vineyard on my native land (about which I had dreamed so much in Riga!).

I didn't take advantage of most of these possibilities. To do so would have meant to sit by and allow my fellow Jews to sacrifice their Jewishness to modern and ultra-modern idols of so-called civilization and progress. Although I was not a Chabadnik by birth, I had some right to call myself an adherent of Chabad. According to my understanding of it, the concept of "Chabadnik" and the state of satiated well-being were incompatible. Finally, there is another reason why I voluntarily condemned myself to a life of chronic lack of sleep, of constantly feeling a catastrophic lack of time.

And this is why. When I arrived at Lod, a young Chabadnik named Betzallel Shif, whom I had known in Russia, told me about an association of religious Jewish intelligentsia from the Soviet Union in Israel. This association had been founded upon the advice of the Lubavitcher Rebbe who thought that people who had struggled to create Jewish homes and Torah education in Russia were duty-bound to continue their efforts after settling in Israel. Rabbi Israel Leibov, Director of Tzeirei Agudat Chabad ("Tzach") in Israel took on the responsibility for creating this association. He entrusted Betzallel to direct it temporarily. Betzallel told me that he had exhausted himself trying to do this, but he lacked sufficient experience and therefore wanted me to head it. A considerable time later, I consented — after long deliberations and consultations with Israel Leibov and his associate, Avroam Godin. I knew the latter from Riga, where for a whole winter in the mid-1960's he had taught me *Chumash* with Rashi's commentaries.

It was clear that this organization was necessary not only for the realization of the fundamental Chabad ideal of Jewish family life and education, but also for the success and continuation of Russian Jewish immigration to Israel. After all, what was it that induced Jews to cut themselves off from their familiar habitats, friends and life routine, if not Jewish consciousness? However, as I have explained earlier, the extent to which this consciousness flowed was so minute among so many Russian Jews that it was enough only to produce an occasional protest or emotional outburst.

Deeper feeling and more substantial knowledge are needed for the long process of absorption into the Land of Israel. Thus, the purpose of this association was to develop Jewish feeling and to give Jewish knowledge to Russian Jews in Israel. To do this, teachers and lecturers had to be found to create serious, academic-level literature on Jewish subjects in good Russian and to deal with all possible psychological and sociological aspects of acclimatizing Russian Jews to their homeland. All this (and more) was to become the range of activities of this association, later to be known as "Shamir" ("Shomrei Mitzvot Yotzei Russia"—The Association of Jewish Religious Professionals from the Soviet Union and Eastern Europe in Israel).

Shamir had incredible difficulties to overcome. There was a shortage of suitable personnel, a catastrophic lack of funds, and an absurd necessity to prove over and over again to the powers-that-be the vital necessity of their supporting Shamir's activities. Now, however, both the Israeli government and the Jewish Agency recognize its importance. Shamir has been undertaking difficult and indeed historic tasks, such as the publication of a Russian translation of the Five Books of Moses with the commentaries of Rashi, Ramban, Ibn-Ezra and others (the first such annotated Russian-Hebrew *Chumash* ever to be printed). It is also preparing new Russian translations of the *Shulchan Aruch* and the *Kuzari*. Gradually, a Russian-language Basic Jewish Library of the classics of Judaism is being created to serve as the cornerstone of Jewish revival and self-education among Russian Jews, on both sides of the Iron Curtain.

43 Hundreds of people turn to Shamir and to me as its chairman. Many come requesting literature or consultation on religious-philosophic subjects, as well as seeking help in finding work, appropriate schools for their

children, loans or even better apartments. Sometimes fathers come looking for a match for their daughters.

The degree of my activity in Shamir grows greater and greater. To my great fortune, a wonderful person who has now become my close friend, Peter Kalms, has entered the Shamir orbit to help me. The Rebbe brought Peter to Shamir. Peter's grandfather emigrated to England three-quarters of a century ago from Russia. For this and for other reasons, Peter became interested in the problems of Russian Jews and began to empathize with them. He made a deep impression on me from our very first encounter. I was still very "green" then in the free world, but I had already managed to form an impression of the typical Jewish businessman-philanthropist. In many cases, the charity of such a philanthropist seemed to be primarily for self-"publicity." His ignorance and lack of desire to understand the cause for which he sometimes gave and sometimes didn't give money was simply appalling.

By that time, I had already attended a few meetings on behalf of Soviet Jewry, which had been conducted according to the unwritten laws of cocktail party games. Everyone made the rounds, exchanging intoxicating compliments, getting carried away with themselves, and gustily eating and drinking, radiating charming smiles and delivering an uninterrupted flow of sheer nonsense.

Peter appeared to be the exact opposite of this stereotype. He genuinely lives through everything he does, feeling its excitement and trying to penetrate into every detail and understand all. He is always ready to perform the most menial task, to take upon himself every possible obligation. His intelligence, competency, quick-wittedness and intuition, combined with unusual accuracy and feeling of responsibility have, to a great extent, secured Shamir's success. He has been an invaluable help to me, and I have tried to follow his example many times.

The course of events has confirmed more and more the importance of the concerns with which Shamir deals. As the miraculous exodus of Soviet Jewry dries up and withers, turning into a far from idealistic emigration settling on five continents, it becomes evident that without real Jewish education, any Jewish undertaking—even the most grand and historic—is doomed to fail. Alas, our ignorance of our roots and the habit of thinking only in materialistic terms hide this simple truth from most of those who consider themselves to be today's captains and helmsmen of the long-suffering Jewish ship.

44   Did Israel live up to my expectations? During the first few months or even the entire first year after I arrived, this frequently-asked question seemed outlandish to me. Drunk with happiness, experiencing unbelievable events, walking in a dream—all these are expressions far too weak to describe the state I was in.

It often happened, though, during that time, that I heard people say that the party leaders and "functionaries" were ready to betray and sell out everybody and everything for the advantage of their careers, party interests and political gain. I heard allegations that a considerable part of the population related hostilely to all that is traditionally, eternally Jewish. Finally, I heard stories of disgusting examples of corruption. However, all these reports evoked in me only irritation and sheer distrust toward the people who told them to me. For me there existed only the holy and unique quality of this cherished and longed-for land. Therefore, even the most sincere criticism sounded slanderous to me. This happy intoxication was so strong that even now, years after our *aliya*, it still makes itself felt.

However, for quite a while now, I have begun to see and realize what is going on and to become aware of the difference between the State of Israel and the Land of Israel, and my heart has begun to bleed. Most difficult of all was to see how secularism and socialism were considered the highest social values. I do not mean the socialism of the prophet Amos but the socialism of (as they say in Hebrew — "May they be separated by a thousand separations") Karl Marx.

The intoxication with socialism in certain circles is so strong that it is considered possible to heedlessly sacrifice anything to fulfill its dogmas. And if it should happen that the demands of socialist principles should conflict with an internal Jewish voice, then it is simply improper to allow the latter to have its say. From my recently accumulated experience I know that what I have just written would probably arouse a storm of indignation from members of the labor parties and applause from associates of the "Herut" party. Therefore, I hasten to explain that I do not belong to Herut, just as I do not belong to the labor parties, since I am convinced that the very division of Jews into parties is wrong. (I do not have in mind here the people belonging to the parties. As individuals, as Jews, they are frequently sympathetic and reasonable.)

Moreover, I must express my complete appreciation and respect for the socialists of the founding generation for their heroism and self-sacrifice and for their amazing achievements in building and defending the country. This, however, does not change the fact that they were tragically mistaken in their ideology and probably could not even guess the disastrous consequences that their world outlook would wreak within a few decades.

More than once I have had occasion to be convinced of the tragedy of the very existence of political parties and, even worse, that part of them — guided by their party ideology and mentality — are in a position of authority to decide questions critical to our people. I also saw that there are neither moral barriers nor logical limits to the endless animosity and strife among the various parties. It is significant that the Hebrew word for party, *miflaga*, comes from the root *pilug* (meaning separation, division). What could be more tragic for our small, persecuted people than internal division and discord?

By the way, before each election to the Knesset, several parties persisted in offering me a place on their list of candidates. In a number of cases a "sure seat" was offered. But it seemed preposterous to align myself with one group of Jews, thus automatically pitting myself in opposition to all other Jews. So naturally I declined.

Far more disturbing to me is the catastrophic national loss of a Jewish frame of mind, of a Jewish world outlook, of our age-old principles and ideas, of feeling the kinship and interdependence of all Jews, and of the formerly well-known Jewish fineness of spirit and mind. For many Israeli Jews, their link with the past, the continuity of the generations, has been lost. The machine of secular-socialist-atheist-cosmopolitan education ruthlessly grinds down the inner core of Jewishness, which miraculously is still reproduced in the souls of Jewish children. This system of education grew out of the views of German and Western European Jewish leaders of the "Enlightenment" — *Maskilim* — who, 150 to 200 years ago started their monstrous experiment to substitute the treasures of the Jewish soul with "universal humanism." After absorbing elements of Russian socialism, this system "enriched" itself with pearls of American didactic thought and the spirit of total permissiveness and unlimited personal freedom. Mastering all this eclectic broth, it then turned into the most banal anti-Semitism, hostile not against Jewish flesh and blood but against the Jewish soul and the Jewish heart.

It is hard to imagine anything stranger than seeing the heirs of the Chosen People — who for more than three thousand years were the bearers and guardians of holiness, justice and human wisdom — turned into such a philistine race, whose heathen cult of the body, pleasure and success is not very modestly covered by the fig-leaf of "progress" and "service to the ideals of all mankind."

Unbearable pain is evoked in me when I think of the crowds on Allenby or Dizengoff streets in Tel Aviv, where among the half-naked girls, daubed-up old women and long-haired males it is hard to detect a Jewish face or Jewish expression in the eyes. It is impossible for me to watch young men and women on television shamelessly declare that they are Israelis, Canaanites, but in no way Jews. It is terrifying to see newspaper kiosks and movie billboards in the Holy Land promoting blown-up pictures of the female body distorted, despiritualized, and degraded to arouse carnal appetites. It is unbearable to realize that all this is happening in *Eretz Hakodesh*. It is even more unbearable to realize that assimilation here is much more dangerous than in other countries where Jews live. In the Diaspora, assimilation ultimately causes the complete separation of an individual Jew or a Jewish family from the body of the Jewish people. Here, in Israel, however, a spiritually degraded Jew is still considered a Jew for the simple reason that he lives in a "Jewish state." Thus, assimilation here becomes not only a personal tragedy. It is devaluating the basic concept of a "Jew" and the "Jewish people."

45 The most valuable quality which has been lost in Israel is not even Jewish intellectual refinement or eternal thirst for knowledge. The most valuable Jewish quality which is decreasing in Israel is the sense of the limits of what is allowed, the feeling of the borders of sin. Traditionally, a Jew always strived to stay away from the forbidden, the immoral and the shameful. Throughout the ages, the Jew tried to preserve the purity of all his actions and thoughts and the holiness of his family and community. "You are a Jew!" "We are Jews!" More than any explanation or moralizing lecture, these words always brought one of our people who was being led astray back to his heritage. It is agonizing to see how this priceless inheritance is vanishing. Although, to be fair, I must note that often I do have the occasion to see the strength of the *mitzvoth* continuing to live in the souls of many whose intellects have tried to disavow them.

How agonizing it is to hear and read in the papers about murder committed by Jews, about Jewish prostitutes, about rape, about cases of robbery and theft, and about strikes sabotaging a war-time economy. However, all this can be attributed to a minority, the dregs of society. Therefore, it is even more terrible to hear of or to see incidents that at first seem much less scandalous. For example, in September of 1975, at the central bus station in Tel Aviv, a teen-ager attacked a man carrying a briefcase containing eighteen thousand *liroth* worth of bank notes. The boy was caught right away, but the briefcase popped open, allowing the bank notes to scatter. When they were collected, it turned out that ten thousand *liroth* had disappeared into the pockets of passers-by. In other words, dozens of chance passers-by turned out to be thieves. A hundred years ago in a remote *shtetl* in the Pale of Settlement, this never could have happened.

Endless sorrow floods the soul when a student, returning from fighting in the Yom Kippur War, says: "I've read in books about Jewish happiness and joy and the beauty of Shabbath, but although I grew up in Israel, I've never had the chance to experience it. I'm not the type who goes to discotheques, and all my entertainment consists of television on weekdays, and on Shabbath — more television."

Or take a very different example. When a cinema shows a film consisting of two entire hours of detailed depiction of nude bodies indulging in sexual acts and refined perversions, the seats are filled up. But when a film about Yanush Korchak comes, then the maximum number of tickets sold for a show is twenty.

It makes you suffocate from helplessness and despair to hear that, upon the advice of foreign didactic-schizophrenics, a course on sex education is being introduced into the schools, where the technique of the sex act is explained to boys and girls through films which demonstrate accordingly. And what can be said about seeing a fourteen-year-old girl taking a contraceptive pill, preparing to go out on a date, while her parents look on with condescension. And it never even occurs to them that there is anything reprehensible in this! What can we expect from our enemies when we ourselves — in the name of alien and depraved theories and in order to gratify our own dissoluteness — mutilate the purity and holiness of our children's souls, uprooting them from the Jewish spirituality, modesty and self-restraint which our forefathers struggled to preserve for centuries? This, O God, is probably the lowest level to which Your will sentenced us to fall for our sins.

46 In Russia I had read about various reform movements in Judaism, but this information remained completely abstract for me. I recollect, however, that one Shabbath during the hardest period of our struggle to get out of the Soviet Union, a young foreigner barged into our apartment. He said he was an American rabbi. Loaded with baggage and cameras, he had come to us by bus. His bald, bare head shone with sweat. All this made us very suspicious. Needless to say, the "rabbi" did not inspire us with the slightest desire to seek his advice or help.

By now I have had the occasion to meet face to face with more of these "experimenters" and "innovators." I have become acquainted with shaven, bare-headed men who devour pork sausage and drive around on Saturday in their Cadillacs, shamelessly calling themselves "rabbis." I have even had the opportunity to see — not in real life, but in a documentary film — a wedding ceremony performed by a "rabbi" and a priest together.

When I think about all these Reform, Conservative, progressive and heaven-knows-what-else movements, countless arguments rooted in the Torah, in historical experience, in philosophy, in logic and common sense come to mind, proving the absurdity of all these sorry innovations. First of all, there is no logical basis for calling these trends religion. As the reformers consider it possible for human beings to change *halacha* (the God-given Jewish law) at will, then there is no place for God in their "doctrine." How can something in which there is no place for God be called religion? It should be called, at most, a cultural movement or social club.

But the simplest and most convincing argument is possibly one which I heard recently from an engineer — a modest and reasonable man. When asked why he doesn't go to the Conservative "temple" near his home, the engineer answered without hesitation: "Once I read Rambam's *Book of Knowledge*. He says that *halacha* can't be changed. You know, the Rambam is good enough an authority for me..." Actually, this man hadn't said anything special, but what immense, unsophisticated truth there was in his words! Oh, if only all of us could feel that "the Rambam is good enough an authority for me."

I must also mention here the compromising Orthodox Jews. With a heavy heart I force myself to do this. Far be it from me to equate the more liberal elements of Orthodox Jewry with Reformism. But I have become convinced (neither quickly nor easily!) that although this tendency toward liberalism does not eliminate any of the tradition, by changing the priorities of certain *mitzvoth* and by relaxing certain restrictions on conduct it has also often allowed people to fall away from Judaism.

I am definitely not referring here to the disgraceful political intrigues that have unfortunately been exposed in the religious parties. I have in mind now only their founding ideology which presumed that young freethinkers would be attracted to Judaism through a lenient attitude. But, alas, life has proven that too many people are crossing the bridge in the wrong direction!

And to my friends of the religious parties (just think what a paradox it is to juxtapose "religion" with "party" when we are actually all one party, the party of Moshe Rabbeinu!) I wish to cry out: "How can you call the present fallen state of our land, this tragedy of the degradation of everything Jewish, the beginning of Messianic redemption? We must love and protect our land and our people with all our heart and all our might and try to bring the coming of the *Mashiach* nearer. But let's not stupefy ourselves by calling darkness light!"

Possibly the greatest tragedy of the modern age is not that the vast majority of Jews, including the most vainglorious intelligentsia, are totally immersed in atheism and scepticism, but that among those who consider themselves to be believers and *shomrei mitzvoth,* there are so few truly possessing simple faith, trusting in God. Rationalism and scepticism are infiltrating more and more into circles considering themselves Orthodox. There are "religious people" who believe in an abstract God, the God of Creation or of History, but who have lost their personal connection with Hashem Who directs the most minute activities in the world. This "half faith" or even "quarter faith" has various manifestations. The believer in such a fractured faith sees the *mezuza* as a beautiful tradition, but neither realizes nor feels that the *mezuza* guards the Jewish home not only figuratively but also literally. Such a person, when talking about his future plans, does not add *"im yirtze Hashem"* (if God wills it) because it seems indecorous to him to display his faith so "primitively." Moreover, he simply does not feel that the realization of his plans depends upon the Almighty. If this person is a political leader dealing, for example, with the inadmissibility of returning territory liberated by Israel during the Six-Day War, then it doesn't enter his head to substantiate his position, whether arguing with Jews or non-Jews, by referring foremost to the fact that this land was given to us by the will of God and that it cannot but be ours.

When a young person doesn't constantly feel the presence of God and doesn't sense a Higher Power is observing his behavior; when he is told that not every *mitzva* and, even more so, not every custom is equally binding and that the words of the Torah can always be taken allegorically — then very soon this youngster starts coming to *shul* in shorts and his *yarmulke* diminishes to the size of a coin, lost in his shoulder-length hair. His *tallith katan* turns into something resembling a baby's bib and then disappears altogether. Soon he starts dancing with girls, and after a while it's not unusual for him to go even further. Alas, what is written here is not theory, but simple observations of life. The Torah neither tolerates nor forgives compromises! The most dangerous innovation of all, though, is to change the Torah from being the basis of life into becoming an isolated part of it.

I must emphasize and stipulate again and again that all the painful examples of alienating and self-deceiving departures from Judaism given here are not meant in any way to slander or harm any individual or group. I have met many admirable people in every aspect of Jewish life who are immeasurably dedicated to the Jewish people. My intention here is strictly to warn my fellow Jews of the dangers incurred by trying to change, compromise or eliminate any of the laws of the Torah. Because the quality of Jewish physical survival depends upon how well each individual Jew daily carries out true Jewish values and precepts, I am just trying to point out inconsistencies and contradictions demanding immediate correction.

47   Every day I meet people here in Israel who are fully prepared to give of themselves, although sometimes they are too shy to openly display this old-fashioned virtue. Often during crisis or times of joy, Jewish light suddenly bursts forth, emerging from our common historical experience of thousands of years, binding the people around me in a precious intimacy. The Jewish soul is indestructible. Sometimes a seemingly insignificant event fills my heart with a happy surprise, when by chance a passenger on the bus

turns around smiling and says "*Shalom*," or a group of first-graders troops by, weighed down by back satchels far too heavy for them — schoolchildren like all other schoolchildren, but with large Jewish eyes. Sometimes a bunch of long-haired, gum-chewing teen-agers in bell-bottoms come at me on the street, just like the most devil-may-care Russian hooligans. Out of habit I cringe, preparing to defend myself, but, instead, suddenly one of them turns to me and politely asks directions how to get somewhere. And the superman arrogance in his eyes fades, and in its place I see the look of my own son.

At such moments everything within me cries out and exults. Wonder and triumph beat on a kettledrum. You are all mine, my own, for better or for worse. You are not always as I wish you to be — may God set you on the right path. But I am part of you, and no one looks at me like a stranger. Do you hear? The officials here can be the rudest bureaucrats (although, to tell the truth, I have not often found them so), but they never, never think about me, "Look at what a kike he is."

And the land is ours, belonging to all of us, eternally so, commanded to all of us and linked to us through the great secrets of the Torah, even though many of us neither understand nor feel this.

In traveling across this land — and hardly a workday goes by that I do not travel at least one hundred kilometers — I feel a tremendous joy. If by some miracle I could suddenly be freed of all my endless obligations, I would prefer not to drive but to walk through this land, feeling her stones beneath my feet, breathing in the scents of her mountains, gardens and deserts, talking with her people, grasping her soul.

But even shuttling along her exhaust-fume-filled highways, I feel connected with my, our, land. Every day newer beauty and additional depths of spirituality are revealed through the modesty of her external appearance, and I love her more and more.

I love her even in the unbearably hot summer days when the

air in the valleys is thick and sticky, when the scents of broiling patches of green are dominated by a strong smell of parched dust. Only on the hills and in the mountains during twilight does the slightly weakening sun allow an invasion of cooling wind which somehow manages to hide and survive.

I love her in the lightning-blazed days of winter rain, when the streets of the cities turn into impassable streams, and even the southernmost stubborn, lifeless "wadis" swell with raging muddy waters.

I love her even more in the blessed weeks of spring when ripening grain of all shades of green play beneath the wind on broad expanses of plowed hills; when the almond trees are dressed in their floral pink and white wedding gowns; when pines modestly flower in the mountains, in every crevice of which, among stones washed by the subsiding rains, shy pink cyclamens blush with downcast eyes into their heart-shaped leaves, while glowing red anemones and majestic blue irises are drawn toward the sun.

Nothing disturbs the cool solemn splendor of the wooded slopes. Only now and then a stone zips down, dislodged by the sure hooves of a gazelle. A lizard rustles. A hoopoe bird, competing with the brightness of the flowers, announces itself. And at the same time along the roadsides and in littered yards, grasses vie in their wildness, flecked with yellow calendulas and ubiquitous, cheerful daisy-like blooms.

I love the cities of my land — disorderly and featureless, but mine. When I approach them at night beneath the unfathomable heaven, under the moon set at an angle strange to northern eyes, the twinkling, flickering lights of the city appear. And it seems to me that the place calls to me, "I am yours, truly yours, enter me."

The very word "desert" is supposedly depressing. I can't say anything about other deserts, but the Judean Desert, the Negev and the Sinai for me are a focus of joy and unspeakable beauty.

It is possible to write without end about the tamarisks

undaunted by the dry winds, about the fabulous magnificence of the cliffs and hills of these deserts with their charming play of color cast in beautiful profusions — from light gold to dark violet, in shades forever changing with the movement of the sun. Songs of praise should be sung to the Negev when its hills, sown with wheat and barley, are dressed in all shades of green. And it makes you marvel how boundless is this land, considered so small in terms of land surveying.

But even more exciting is the fact that all these scenes are perceived — so to speak — in four dimensions. To the three dimensions perceived by the eyes is added a perspective of history unfolding in time. The eye searches for the tent of Avraham Avinu in the Negev hills. A mental image is formed of this great man, whose greatness lay in the full submission of his will to the word of the Creator.

In the damp caves of Ein Gedi or on the slopes of the Hebron hills, among the terraced vineyards and ancient olive trees, I hardly dare to breathe as I wait, entranced, to encounter King David — young, fearless and passionate, enraptured with his love for God, which he expressed in the Psalms.

And it seems that the *kohanim* are walking the Temple Mount in their priestly robes. And it appears that Ruth, the Moabitess who accepted the Torah with all her heart, is carefully treading the golden sun-burnt field of stubble, gathering sheaves.

And where shall I find the words to write about you, Jerusalem! Every time I excitedly realize that I am turning the last bend on the road approaching the Holy City, suddenly the sun-lit brightness of the Jerusalem stone blinds my eyes. I long to slow down and examine myself again: am I ready to meet the center of the universe, the time axis of world history?

48 My attitude toward this land and my yearning for it are just as reverential as they were five or ten years ago, in spite of the unfortunate superficialities about which I wrote previously. And my appreciation for this land is heightened when I find myself in other countries. In recent years I have traveled a lot, covering five continents. Whenever I am abroad, I miss my homeland even more — her people and landscape, her charm and tension, all created precisely to serve as background for events of cosmic significance.

It is not surprising, then, that I am torn apart when I read in the papers or actually see with my own eyes cases of monstrous moral degradation. And our national economic and political degeneration, which at first seems to be an independent phenomenon, is actually a deep result of this fundamental moral degradation.

The attitudes, values and education absorbed from childhood first and foremost mold the character of a human being, whether he is a simple craftsman or a government minister. Thus, when people complain about the helplessness of their government, the only advice to give them is, "Look at yourselves. The ministers of the government are exact reflections of yourselves. Even if they were all Solomons, they would not be able to transcend the limits of your miserable, all-is-allowed, nihilistic beliefs. In reward for having fastidiously learned what you were taught and having preserved democracy, you get a government that resembles yourselves."

I want to run out into the street, grab the first people I see and shout:

Brothers! Brothers! Wake up! Aren't you convinced that your experiment of an atheistic Israel has failed? Can it be that you don't yet sufficiently realize that it is possible for Jews to live on this land only by keeping the laws of the Torah — because otherwise the land will spew us forth? Maybe you haven't had enough wars and suffering? Maybe you still imagine that Marx is going to bring you prosperity? Or that skillful diplomacy can convince the world to moderate its anti-Semitism? If you don't accept the Holy Torah, then how can you firmly believe that this land is ours, from time immemorial and forever, categorically ours? You must finally understand that peace will not be brought to the Holy Land by strength of arms alone, because the real question is: does our behavior make us deserve a peaceful life in our land? Are we worthy of it? For the sake of our children, let us finally put an end to the pitiful game of "sophistication," covering up our submission to alien paganism. He Who more than three thousand years ago gave us the choice between a blessing and a curse is still waiting patiently with fatherly love, urging us to "Choose life!"

So let us choose life. Let us entrust our fate to the Almighty. Let us cleanse our homes from all that is alien and borrowed imitation, hostile and crude. Let us make way for goodness and holiness in the souls of our children! Bearing the weight of war, our youth have been robbed and deprived too long of the simple and wise human joys of a Jewish Sabbath, of Jewish holidays, of the Jewish cycle of life.

Just remember what it is like here during the one day of the year when no one yet dares to separate the Jews from God — Yom Kippur. (I don't mean the Yom Kippur when the terrible war broke out on us.) People become attentive and sensitive, more patient, kinder. Strangers greet each other quietly on the street. Something invisible, long forgotten, descends upon us all. Suddenly Jews sense their commitment to one another, their commitment to the Jewish people and to the Almighty Who chose them from all other peoples. Cars don't rush around, driven by people intoxicated by feeling their own power increased by mechanical engines. The air — ordinarily suffocating with dust and fumes—is quiet, clean and fragrant with the aroma of the earth.

Oh, if only we could learn to behave like that every Shabbath! What a gift it would be for our children, who now at best are provided with immoral television programs and movies and at worst with discotheques and night clubs! How rightly did our sages say that redemption will come when all of Israel observes the Sabbath two times in a row as it is commanded to be kept. Just two Sabbaths!

49   Thus do I want to cry out to my brothers, to entreat and implore them. And thus do I try to cry out, entreat and implore at the countless meetings, lectures, and discussions which for the past three years have occupied almost all of my evenings and many of my days, too.

My time is as tight as a drawn bowstring. The smallest unforeseen delay, half an hour not spent as planned, can ruin my schedule for a whole week. Unexpected guests, even the most welcome ones, throw me into a panic. Alas, the people around me often cannot understand the tension of my timetable and are thus offended when I am not in a position to devote enough time to them. I steal time from my research and from my family to rush to Tel Aviv, Ashdod, Haifa, Jerusalem, Dimona. I almost catastrophically fall asleep behind the wheel on the way to meet with students, schoolchildren, professors, soldiers, officers, kibbutzniks. Sometimes it happens that I appear in three different cities in one day, while still spending a few hours in between at my magnetohydrodynamics laboratory at Beersheva University, delivering a lecture to students on turbulence, and fulfilling every possibly imaginable kind of duty connected with my dozens of academic and social responsibilities.

It weighs heavily on my heart that Beersheva, the capital of the Negev and a well-organized, rapidly developing city, is spiritually a desert. And thus, in addition to all my other activities, I have taken it upon myself to establish Chabad educational institutions for the children and the general public of Beersheva, and especially for its university students. With God's help and the blessings of the Rebbe, gardens are being cultivated to make the desert bloom.

And invitations and letters keep coming in. And the telephone keeps ringing. From students, schoolchildren, women's organizations, parents' committees, new immigrants . . .

Every time I decide to decline the next request, but every next time I don't have the heart to refuse. How can I not give way to the temptation to try one more time to change these people — my brothers who have thoughtlessly deprived themselves and their children, living as if there had never been a Ba'al Shem Tov or an Ari Hakadosh; as if the Rambam had never written his books or as if Rashi's commentaries had never been published; as if the great Tana'im Rabbi Akiva and Rabbi Shimon bar Yochai had never devoted their lives for us, or as if Moshe Rabbeinu had never led us through the desert and HaKadosh Baruch Hu had never given us the Torah on Mount Sinai? If five or ten years ago in Russia I had been asked to lecture on the significance of Judaism in the twentieth century, I would have dropped everything to go, no matter what the distance or what the cost . . . So, I go.

I go because I know that Notke or any real Chassid would go. I go because I must tell my brothers that something inadmissible is happening: the People of the Book is turning into a people of television. I go despite the fact that I know that in an audience of one or two hundred people, possibly — with much luck   my talk will influence one soul. Everyone will listen attentively, many will even agree, possibly even applaud and ask questions. But only one sole person is likely to truly think about what he heard, consider it as affecting himself personally and arrive at some practical conclusions and decisions. And if I don't have any luck, then not even that one lone individual will be there.

Yet, our sages teach us that to save one soul is the same as saving the whole world. And who knows — a drop of water eats the stone away . . . Therefore they say in Chabad: "Man's job is to create. But for him to succeed in creating — that's God's job."

There is a parable that on the eve of Yom Kippur an eminent old rabbi met an elderly non-observant Jew. The rabbi talked with the man about the approaching Day of Judgment. They argued and debated for two hours. Before parting, the rabbi asked: "So you will fast tomorrow?" His counterpart replied, "No. I've never done this before in my life and I'm too old to change my habits." The rabbi's students, who had been waiting, irritated and impatient, for the end of what seemed to them to be a meaningless argument, asked: "Teacher, what is the sense of spending so much time on the eve of the most awesome day of the year in uselessly admonishing an old fool instead of devoting yourself to higher matters and *teshuva*?"

"You are mistaken, my children," the rabbi answered. "I have no doubt that before this man departs from this world, he will remember our discussion and say in his heart: 'It's too bad that I didn't listen and fast.' And you should know that the repentance of a Jew deserves two hours of the time of even the busiest person."

50   In delivering my talks I have been invaluably helped by the knowledge gained from my concentrated "private appointments" or *yechiduth* with the Rebbe. Most especially has he enriched my understanding of science and Torah and their interrelationship.

The unavoidable discussion of science with the Rebbe at first distressed me because in *yechiduth*, more than in any other situation, I wanted to be cut off from routine, to be raised up to touch, even though only slightly, the true heights of the spirit. But no, every time that I came to the Rebbe, after a benevolent welcome he would put aside my last letter of questions requesting his opinions and advice. And with an apologetic smile of rebuke he would say, "Again you don't write anything about your work. Let's hear first what's new there." And thus would start a new discussion about secular university affairs, about new experiments in my laboratory, scientific articles and the unfinished manuscript of my new textbook.

After several such meetings, I not only got used to discussing science with the Rebbe, but I also developed my own explanation as to why he chooses this topic of conversation with me. First of all, everyone lucky enough to have ever met with the Rebbe knows that he adjusts his language, vocabulary and style to suit the background and level of his guest. The Rebbe can intersperse his Yiddish with Russian, German, French, English or modern Hebrew idiom. From one guest to another, he can switch from journalistic jargon to refined philosophic debate, from the mundane concerns of a craftsman or merchant to the cosmic heights of Talmud and Kabbala. With a writer the Rebbe discusses the latest books; with a military leader, the most advanced weapons; with a businessman, stock exchange news; with a doctor, breakthroughs in medicine; with an engineer, the efficiency of a new instrument he is designing. Everyone feels at home talking to the Rebbe in his own familiar language and of his own interests.

If anyone were to ever eavesdrop on my *yechiduth*, he would be hard put to believe that from the office of the Rebbe, the *tzaddik*, the personification of Torah, leader of Chassidim, and teacher and advisor to thousands upon thousands of Jews, emanate expressions like "advantages of direct contact heat transfer in liquids . . . ," "suppression of turbulence in a magnetic field . . . ," "difficulties of separating phases while preserving the kinetic energy of a liquid . . . ," "the budget for buying a new thermoanemometric system...," "the composition of the organizing committee of the Conference of Magnetohydrodynamics...." And all this in Yiddish, with the scientific terms partly in English, partly in Russian. Even I myself sometimes forget that I am not participating in an actual university consultation. But the Rebbe's immediate, unfaltering evaluation of every situation and his conclusions instantly recall me to reality and remind me in whose presence I stand.

The attention which the Rebbe gives to people is so intensely focused and empathetic that it is as if he clothes himself in the personality of his guest. And since the guest and the circumstances of his life are changing between any two visits to the Rebbe, in every additional encounter the visitor discovers something uniquely new in the Rebbe.

Everyone is always amazed at how expert the Rebbe is in any specialized field, but how many people marvel at the fact that the Rebbe is talking with each distinguished specialist about one and the same thing? For the truth is that the Rebbe discusses only one thing with his endlessly diverse guests: the indivisible unity of Israel, the Torah and the Almighty. He talks of illimitable love for fellow Jews — especially for Jewish children — the chosen dwelling place for the Divine spark here in the lowest of worlds. Focusing on the individual interests of his guests, the Rebbe is then able to explain fundamental concepts of Judaism and to awaken people to realizing them in their own daily lives.

This is why the Rebbe has chosen in my own case natural science as the basis upon which to teach the refined and exact structure of Jewish thought and to map out instructions for action. Although the publication of new scientific articles, the start of new research or a fundamental change in existing experiments may result from a *yechiduth*, the Rebbe's every word clearly hints that these were not his intentions. There is only one motive for the Rebbe's involvement in secular matters: "In all your ways know the Lord."

Furthermore, the Torah teaches that action is what counts.

This means carrying out the *mitzvoth*. Thus, everything that can help to disseminate and to fulfill observance of *mitzvoth* is good. If my career, my place in the scientific world, my status in the eyes of young people and my contact with them help to enable more Jewish children to receive a Jewish education, more Jewish families to discover the harmony and meaning of living by the Torah, then the success of an experiment in magnetohydro-dynamics acquires real value in accord with the Jewish scale of values. Putting it plainly — the Rebbe wants the Jewish youngster to start putting on *tefillin* after hearing the university professor talk about science and Torah. And then all the professor's activities will acquire meaning. The inroads that the demands of his profession make on his Torah study then become justified.

In addition to this practical approach, there is a deeper plane on which the Rebbe talks with me about science. Often in the small hours of the morning after several intense hours of exchange, the Rebbe suddenly prompts, "Certainly this time, too, you have questions about science and Chassidism that are bothering you. Ask!" And so I feverishly hunt among the questions that have been assailing me or that my lecture audiences ask me. The Rebbe answers every question in detail, with numerous digressions into Chassidism: Kabbala on the one hand and the most exotic problems of modern science on the other.

I would never dare bring a tape recorder to *yechiduth* or take notes in the Rebbe's presence. Therefore I must make a tremendous effort to remember. Alas, my memory is not capable of retaining all the details of the wisdom and knowledge which spring forth. I shall mention here only a few of the subjects upon which the Rebbe has expounded to me in private. He has given me a general evaluation of the natural sciences from the Torah point of view. He has probed the absolute truth of the scientific-type of knowledge found in the Torah. He has weighed the advantages versus the detrimental factors found in examining the so-called contradictions between Torah and science. He has judged the authenticity of scientific speculations, particularly those which are extrapolated into the distant past. He has deliberated on the informative value of the sciences to Torah study and has discussed the meaning of miracles. He has discussed the connection between nerve impulses and consciousness and will; the structure of time and space vis à vis the Theory of Relativity; free will and Providence; proof of the Revelation at Mount Sinai; the usefulness of scientific examples and analogies to bring young people to identify with Torah . . .

I shall try to convey here only a few of the most characteristic examples of the Rebbe's amazingly unique approach to the problems of science and Torah. As I am relying solely on my memory, unaided by exact notes, inevitably there will be mistakes in the details recounted here from the Rebbe's vast range of learning.

51 Perhaps I should begin with the Rebbe's opinion that it is intolerable for a Jew whose profession is in the sciences to be praised as "a great scientist and, by the way, a believing Jew who lives by the *mitzvoth* of the Torah." This is a terrible recommendation. Judaism cannot be "by the way." It must be the source, the basis. Everything else should be a result of this source of life. A Jewish scientist must strive to be described as "a God-fearing Jew, observing the strict as well as the easy *mitzvoth*, who, by the way, is a great scientist."

In this clear and constant consciousness of the essential versus the non-essential and of the fine line between them lies the very basis of the Rebbe's perception and outlook. Living by the Torah does not mean learning and comprehending it abstractly. Moreover, it does not mean merely adjusting decisions and actions to fit into the instructions of the Torah. The meaning of living by the Torah is that the purpose and content of one's day is literally derived first of all from the meaning which each day has in Torah. Only after actualizing the concrete instructions of the Torah in one's daily life can political events and practical world considerations be taken into account, as they must be.

From his unified, comprehensive view of the world, the Rebbe also formulates his attitude to the natural sciences and their value. Like all other of God's creations, science was created to serve holiness. Whether something actually serves holiness depends on who uses it and under which conditions. For example, explosives can help obtain natural treasures from the earth or they can kill people. Even atomic energy can be a boon. But it also has the potential to exterminate humanity, God forbid. This depends on how man, exercising his freedom of choice, decides to use it.

Science per se is neutral. Potentially it can and ultimately it must lead toward a deeper comprehension of Creation and the Creator. Thus, if properly understood, it can bring a Jew to a more complete life based on *mitzvoth*.

The same can be said about technological progress. For example, radio and television in themselves are neither good nor bad. If these media are used for disseminating lies and encouraging animalistic inclinations, introducing concepts alien to Judaism into the minds of children, or simply "killing time" at the expense of Torah study and good deeds — then both radio and television are absolutely evil. But when these instruments are used to teach Torah, to bring back errant Jews — then radio and TV are absolutely good. Moreover, radio waves broadcasting a Torah lesson literally "fill" material space with the spirit of God's Torah.

Likewise the Rebbe does not criticize the study and advancement of the sciences per se. But criticism is evoked the moment that these studies replace or impair Torah study or *mitzva* observance, the moment they swell a Jew's head so that he forgets his place and purpose. This is why the Rebbe does not encourage a young man to enter the university. Furthermore, the universities—especially the student dormitories—are dens of physical and spiritual degeneration.

Although the Rebbe has no criticism against science as a pursuit in itself, he rejects any apologizing for or compromising of Torah in order to resolve questions about so-called contradictions between Torah and science. Often the supposed contradiction lies in the distant past, for example, in connection with the age of the universe, the theory of evolution, etc. Here, as the Rebbe demonstrates, science has nothing to contribute. All the so-called scientific data in connection with the above-mentioned problems are in reality results of scientifically invalid extrapolations over huge periods of time, i.e. they are simply speculations.

But there are also cases in which the phenomena under question relate to the contemporary world. I asked the Rebbe about a number of such cases where it seems at first glance that contemporary science denies the possibility of some phenomenon mentioned in the Torah or gives an explanation in contradiction to the Torah view. In every one of the cases that I brought to his attention, the Rebbe demonstrated that confusion is caused either by a lack of understanding of how to evaluate and interpret indirect observations (which are very far from being objective knowledge) or because some individuals cannot comprehend that the fact that something has never been observed does not constitute proof of its non-existence. Assumptions based on such "proofs" actually block the progress of science. And such perverted logic, the Rebbe says, is as "valid" as the distorted logic of the once-popular joke in which a boy convinces his friend that the wireless has existed in their village for centuries. How does he know? He's dug and dug in the yards and gardens and still hasn't found any telegraph wire.

The Rebbe stresses the point that the simple, literal meaning of the words of the Torah is always binding. Grave damage has been caused by attempts past and present to "smooth out" people's inner confusion by claiming that the words of the Torah do not have to be understood in their simple, literal meaning. This is an especially dangerous claim when the matters under discussion pertain to practical *halacha*.

It is unacceptable, for instance, to doubt the imperatively literal meaning of the six days of Creation. Days — not ages! Because the six days are the basis for keeping the seventh as the Sabbath — the basis for the entire concept of Shabbath.

A person of strong faith is not bothered by seeming contradictions between the Torah view and what is called the scientific view, because the basic assumption of his faith is that the Torah is absolutely and eternally true. But if other people are bothered by what seems to them to be a contradiction, there is no need to evade such questions, and it actually becomes necessary to examine the problem in a detailed and serious way to avoid confusion.

When confronted with any such seeming contradictions one should keep in mind that experimental science is not able in principle to prove the *impossibility* of any event. Science can only discuss something that has actually been observed and the *probability* of other occurrences. But from this one cannot deduce the impossibility of something which has not yet been successfully observed.

Incidentally, today the probability approach to phenomena prevails in science, particularly in thermodynamics, molecular physics, quantum mechanics, etc. This approach has replaced the concept of an "impossible phenomenon" with the concept of "phenomena of low probability." It does not mean, though, that we should take this idea to the extreme and claim that the miracles mentioned in the Torah weren't supernatural miracles at all, but rather natural phenomena of low probability. The basis of our Torah is that Hakadosh Baruch Hu directly supervises the world and determines the course of every event and phenomenon. Upon this is based, among other things, our understanding of the *mitzva* of prayer. The prayer of a Jew is not only an expression of feelings of gratitude to God and admiration of His greatness, but it can actually influence the course of events in the world according to the requests and desires expressed in it, to the degree that this is the will of God.

It is impossible therefore for a Torah Jew to agree with Laplace, who claimed that if given the knowledge of the precise position of all the atoms in the universe and all the forces acting on them, he would be able in principle to calculate mathematically the future of the entire world. This kind of determinism is unacceptable to twentieth-century science, which is based in great part on statistics and probability. For completely different reasons Laplace's determinism is also unacceptable to the Jew who knows that God creates the world every moment, sustaining and directing its entirety, down to the smallest details. The Jew knows that whether extrapolation of laws deduced from observations made yesterday and today will be correct tomorrow depends upon the will of the Creator.

The Torah perception of the universe excludes any fortuity since every event happens only with the knowledge and will of the Creator. Although it is true that modern science can no longer consider miracles described in the Torah as impossible, it is wrong to view extraordinary events or miracles as natural events of extremely low probability. The Torah unequivocally explains that miracles are *supernatural* events, which occurred only because God willed that the natural order of things be violated.

When I asked the Rebbe once what the Torah says about the possibility of extraterrestrial life, his response was especially characteristic. The possibility of life existing on other planets, replied the Rebbe, is not denied by the Torah. The Talmud mentions such a possibility, but not the possibility of other civilizations of intelligent creatures. According to the Torah, only creatures possessing free will can be categorized as intelligent beings. And free choice is granted and realized only by the Torah. If there were intelligent beings somewhere else in the universe, then they would have to have a Torah. But if they did have a Torah, it could not be one other than ours since our Torah is the Torah of truth, and there is only one truth. However these hypothetical creatures could not have our Torah, because the giving of the Torah to the Jewish people is described in fine detail. Great attention is given to these details, which have the profoundest meaning and are necessary for the understanding of the Torah itself. Thus we must conclude that from a Jewish point of view the existence of extraterrestrial civilizations is impossible.

This answer is particularly characteristic of the Rebbe because the conclusion in the scientific realm is taken entirely from the Torah. The conclusion is based on absolute, unlimited belief in the Torah and also on the concept that the universe and all events therein are secondary to and actually derived from Torah.

52 Once I asked the Rebbe whether he means to say that it is necessary to examine and judge scientific conclusions in the light of the Torah rather than simply ignoring the claims about contradictions between Torah and science. The Rebbe answered that it is necessary to explain how scientific data comes to terms with Torah knowledge, because there are people who need such an explanation. The correct explanation could remove confusion and worry from their hearts.

The Rebbe added that in this respect the approach of the Rambam represents an excellent example. The Rambam demonstrated the key to understanding the proper place of science with relation to Torah, i.e. that "All the works of God are for His sake." Since in addition to his greatness in Torah the Rambam also had an encyclopedic knowledge of philosophy and the natural sciences, he found it necessary to also use these for serving God. His major work was the highly revered and authoritative *Mishneh Torah* (*Hayad Hachazaka*), but he also found it necessary to write *The Guide to the Perplexed*, dealing with philosophy and science. He discussed them in such a way that he made them serve the highest purposes.

It is characteristic that even the first part of Rambam's *Yad Hachazaka* — which is actually the earliest code of Jewish law — is called the "Book of Knowledge." In this introduction, the Rambam shows how and to what limits the human intellect is able to comprehend and cognize the Creator. In other words, it is possible to say that in the realm of knowledge of the physical universe, he prepares the ground for learning spiritual subjects — *mitzvoth*, the detailed *halachoth* discussed in the subsequent thirteen parts of his *Mishneh Torah*.

This progression, namely from physical to spiritual, can be observed in the fulfillment of many *mitzvoth*. Although the *mitzvoth* express the revealed will of God and their meaning and content are purely spiritual, their fulfillment demands preparation in the material realm. For example, if the Almighty had wanted to, He certainly could have created complete ready-made *tefillin* for us to place upon our arm and forehead every morning. But this is not the case. The craftsman must prepare the boxes, straps and parchment, the *sofer* has to write the *parshioth*, and the Jew buying them must do so with hard-earned money. The same holds for the *ethrog*. Instead of waking up on the first morning of Succoth to find an *ethrog* in his hand, the Jew must expend time, effort and considerable money before the holiday to seek out a good *ethrog*. Similarly, for some Jews the clarification of natural sciences from the point of view of Torah can serve as a preparation in the sphere of the physical for their acceptance of the Torah and *mitzvoth* upon themselves.

The Rebbe's uncompromising view on the need to follow the simple, literal, direct meaning of the Torah especially pertains to the halachic content of the Torah. If a certain book is recognized and accepted as a halachic work (the criteria for which are put forth in the Torah), then every word and letter in it must be respected as binding as the Law of Moses from Sinai. A classic example of such a halachic work is the Rambam's *Yad Hachazaka*. We are not bound, however, to accept absolutely the literal meaning of scientific-type information contained in non-halachic books like the Rambam's *Guide to the Perplexed* or Yehuda Halevy's *Kuzari*. There is no contradiction in the fact that both the *Yad Hachazaka* and the *Guide to the Perplexed* were written by the Rambam, because the Rambam wasn't, so to say, exactly the same Rambam when he wrote the *Yad Hachazaka* and when he wrote the *Guide to the Perplexed*. Indeed, Moshe Rabbeinu wasn't the same Moshe Rabbeinu when he taught Torah as when he ate. (But of course the way that Moshe Rabbeinu ate only remotely resembled the way that a simple Jew eats.)

53 In keeping with the Chassidic principle that every object and phenomenon which we see and hear must be used to strengthen our worship of God, the Rebbe makes wide use of examples from science and technology to teach the essence of Judaism and the Torah and to explain what the purpose and behavior of a Jew ought to be.

The modern age of science and technology itself was predicted in the Zohar. The Zohar says that in the sixth century of the sixth millennium from the creation of the world (5500 in the Jewish calendar or 1740 in the non-Jewish calendar), the wellsprings of knowledge, including non-Jewish knowledge, will be opened. (Non-Jewish knowledge, i.e. the natural sciences, is called "external," as it is outside the "internal" knowledge of the

Torah. This description applies even more if this type of knowledge is not used to worship God.) The Zohar's prediction refers to the outburst of scientific and technological progress of the past few hundred years, progress which brings us towards the state of "the world being full of the knowledge of God," as it will be in the Messianic age. We mentioned above the example of radio waves carrying a Torah lesson and thus filling material space with the words of God. Modern physics supplies us with another example: in its conclusion about the equivalency of mass and energy, it demonstrates the unity of the Creation, and this gives man an indication of the absolute unity of the Creator.

Modern science and technology can also provide images or parables for a better understanding of the Torah. For instance, the Rebbe uses computer technology to make the following example:

The operating principle and structure of the computer are based upon the sum total results of many years' work in mathematics, electronics and other branches of science and technology. The computer does not create new knowledge — it only elaborates upon information conveyed to it according to certain general principles, producing meaningful results ranging from specific to general, the results of which can be applied to various areas of science and technology. Theoretically, all the work produced by a computer could be done by a human being armed with pencil and paper, but it would take months, perhaps years to complete a single assignment. Moreover, if a mistake were to slip into the hand-made calculation — which is very likely — the entire calculation would have to be done over again.

In today's computer society no intelligent human being would even consider solving any concrete problem by first re-inventing computer technology. On the contrary, anyone can directly benefit from the tried and proven methods of computer programming and data processing without re-proving the theories, formulas and algorithms and without rechecking the hardware structure and internal operations of the particular computer being used. Computer users place absolute trust in the scholars who developed computer theory and in the engineers who constructed the computers.

In contrast to this, many Jews think that they must use their own heads to clarify everything rationally — from the beginning. They hear about Torah, the *mitzvoth*, *halacha* and Jewish life, but they don't want to rely upon the authority, knowledge, experience and work of the great Torah sages. They don't want to benefit from the *Shulchan Aruch*, which was prepared for their simple and easy use. "After we have become orientated in everything by ourselves, after we've checked, proven and argued it out," they say, "then maybe we'll start living by the Torah, putting on *tefillin* and keeping Shabbath." Isn't it clear that such people are putting themselves into a situation far more ridiculous than the hypothetical fool who has access to a computer but who spends years doing calculations because he refuses to use the computer until he himself has determined how the machine works and how each program in the machine was developed?

The Jewish principle "First we will do and then we will hear and understand" does not prohibit the *mitzva* of study and achievement. On the contrary, it encourages learning. But study must be preceded by deeds based on the experience and knowledge of our forefathers and Sages of blessed memory — the "experts" of the Torah.

There is another lesson which the Rebbe finds in the example of the computer. As has already been mentioned, sometimes the results of electronic computations are so general that it is possible to use them in several different areas of science and technology. Sometimes a computer program designed to solve a differential equation describes simultaneously several phenomena of dissimilar physical natures. If an additional phenomenon is discovered which fits the same type of differential equation, then the same program can be used for calculations by simply changing the parameters and boundary conditions. Similarly, the *Shulchan Aruch* gives general rules, a general program and general solutions which are applicable in all ages, regardless of changes in external conditions.

Another of the Rebbe's examples is taken from the interest in solar energy caused by the energy crisis. "What is the unique quality of the sun," asks the Rebbe, "which makes everyone consider it a blessing? It is, of course, its capacity to radiate ("to give light to the earth" — as the first chapter of Genesis says). What would happen if the sun had the same temperature, the same energy, but did not radiate or give heat? Indeed there are such stars, called black holes (their existence is, incidentally, mentioned in the Talmud), the force of attraction of which is so strong that not even one light ray can depart from them. If the sun were such a star, whom would it interest then? Of what use would the sun be if it were a black hole? So it is with the Jew whose primary function is to put forth light, to radiate, to better his fellow man through the *mitzva* of *ahavath Yisrael.* Without this, he would turn into a black hole, when he was created to be a sun."

54   The Rebbe's Jewish philosophy of science may be (to the best of my knowledge and understanding) summed up as follows:

1) Objective scientific knowledge, if properly used, can strengthen faith. Thus, for instance, natural sciences demonstrate unequivocally the unity of the very diverse Creation which has its single source in One God.

2) Exaggerated admiration for anything labeled scientific is most dangerous and converts science into an object of idolatry.

3) Many of the conclusions in science are based on interpreting more or less direct observations and measurements. How adequate and objective these interpretations are usually remains an open question, especially when the subject of the scientific

research lies beyond direct sensory perception. This can happen either because of the remoteness of the subject in space (and even more so in time!) or the smallness of its size, or because its nature makes it imperceptible in principle. In all these cases, the question of objectivity cannot be checked without making even more assumptions.

4) The conceptions, interpretations, and theories of science are constantly changing and alternating between divergent views, with no indication that they will ever arrive at significant agreement on the truth. Thus, often that which is called a theory has a cognitive value corresponding at best to a hypothesis.

5) The acceptance of the assertion that a phenomenon which has not yet been observed does not exist means freezing science to the level corresponding to the moment when this assertion was made.

6) Any judgment about events or objects in the distant past (beyond the time in which related research was carried out) — like any extrapolation extending far from the interval of research — has nothing in common with science and is in fact pure speculation. The classic example of this is "scientific" speculation on the age of the universe.

7) If any seeming contradiction between Torah and science cannot be satisfactorily resolved immediately, at this time there is no reason for panic, or for, God forbid, a Jew to be repelled by Torah and *mitzvoth*. Nothing can be more dangerous than setting a deadline for finding an explanation, since this leads to self-deception out of haste and not to truth.

All of the above-mentioned show the absurdity of placing speculations (not objective scientific knowledge!) against the eternal, unchanging truth of the Torah. This pertains to Torah discussion of the natural consequence of things. As to the cases where the Torah describes the supernatural, the miraculous, it would be even more foolhardy to try to define the supra-rational in rational categories or to discuss supernatural phenomena on the grounds of analyses of nature.

The Rebbe also shows how doubt and disbelief are often generated by subconscious attempts to attribute human logic, thought and attitudes to God. This is why, for example, the Copernican conception of the solar system so triumphantly captured people's belief: it demanded fewer corrections for the description of planet movement than the Ptolemaic conception. But think about it: Is there any basis or justification to the assumption that God constructs the universe in a manner that will seem the most simple to human reason? Human concepts about economy, optimality and simplicity have nothing in common with the Divine act of Creation because man is limited and finite whereas God is infinite and absolutely unrestricted. In the natural world created by God, extravagance (from a human point of view) is a universal phenomenon — extending from the energy radiated by the sun to the semination of plants and animals.

Continuing along this line, the Rebbe has an analogy which explains why so many people are attracted to Darwinism: Suppose that you had to create the world with its multitudinous life forms. Suppose also that you can choose between two ways of doing this. The first is to create each species, each individual separately. The second way is to create matter, then assign it laws of development, and from there on have everything go by itself. Which would you choose? Any normal human being would choose the second. He would be afraid to even contemplate "engineering" and constructing billions of organisms, each one separately. Thus, when considering the Divine Creation, people subconsciously thrust their own human criteria on God. But the Almighty has warned us that "My thoughts are not your thoughts."

All of the above relates to the Rebbe's Jewish interpretation of science. In addition to this, he has given much practical advice to scientists, helping them to develop specific aspects of science. There have been many cases where the Rebbe has found basic mistakes in the professional articles of physicists, microbiologists, mathematicians, and psychologists and has instructed them how to correct the error.

Several years ago, shortly after starting to develop a magnetohydrodynamic system to convert solar energy into electrical energy, I had the privilege to meet with the Rebbe again in *yechiduth*. At once he started to interrogate me about my new invention, delving in depth into the technical details.

Upon hearing my replies to his questions, he immediately brought my attention to two circumstances. First he said that if the velocity of the two-phase flow was really as I had indicated, then the efficiency factor received was too low. Secondly he pointed out that through storing solar heat during the day and converting it into electricity during the cold Negev nights, it would be possible to take advantage of the special climatic properties of the Negev to increase by approximately a third the amount of electrical energy produced. It turned out that the Rebbe's two comments were absolutely correct. I found my mistake in calculating the efficiency factor only two years later. The second suggestion is to be applied in further stages of the project. Surprisingly, of all the many experts with whom I consulted at length about this project, nobody thought of the points which the Rebbe clarified instantaneously after hearing a five-minute briefing.

Such and much other advice which the Rebbe has given on scientific research work in the most diverse fields cannot be explained merely by the fact that he holds a diploma from the Sorbonne and a few other universities. The explanation to this phenomenon is more likely connected to a comprehensive spiritual vision of the world, a vision mirrored through the Torah and feeling the constant presence of the Creator, a vision wherein the material world is but a pale reflection of the spiritual worlds. This phenomenal insight is also greatly explained by the Rebbe's ability and desire to enter entirely into the problems bothering his guests, whoever they may be.

Much has been written about the Rebbe's advice on medical

problems. His medical advice is usually based on a deep esteem for the opinions of doctors and experts. But sometimes the Rebbe's advice directly opposes these opinions. Against the consensus of doctors, for example, the Rebbe has prevented quite a number of abortions, and, in all cases known to me personally, healthy and perfect Jewish babies were born.

55 There are so many things I want to tell my audiences — about everything that I went through searching for my world outlook and all the thinking I did during those years. Chassidism has taught me to see the deep interconnections of all phenomena. Finally freed from the wretched framework of rationalistic and deterministic thought, I can honestly say that not only do I understand but I also deeply feel the unity of this world in God. I can now realize that the countless distinctions between things and events are cancelled within the Infinite Light of Hashem. I understand the direct correlation of all the things and events in the universe with the letters and words of the Torah. Chassidism has taught me to see their total interrelationship with the will of the Creator.

And this is the key to understanding why fulfilling the *mitzvoth* of the Torah — written in the same letters and words out of which the material world is created — is literally a stronger weapon than tanks and planes and missiles in defending ourselves from both the physical and spiritual threats of the non-Jewish world. As the Lubavitcher Rebbe said recently: our people always have been and still remain like a sheep surrounded by seventy wolves. However, the sheep can resist the wolves only so long as he trusts more in the Almighty than in any material means of defense (the importance of which no one can deny), and therefore God protects it. The current tragedy is that the sheep imagines himself a wolf, not needing Divine protection and not realizing that even if he succeeds in becoming a wolf, he will be still only one wolf against seventy.

It isn't easy to explain this to audiences saturated in materialism, but I try to convince them over and over again. I try first of all to make them stop thinking that "Faith is impossible in our times." I attempt to get an answer to the question: "Why was your grandfather a believing Jew who practiced the *mitzvoth* and studied Torah, but you aren't? Perhaps you have discovered something new that justifies your departure from the tradition of your grandfather and great-grandfathers that makes you better than they?"

I have never heard a reasonable answer to this question. People say things like: "My grandfather didn't have electricity." "He didn't watch television." They've even said: "My grandfather didn't have a modern toilet."

Then I attempt to clarify what — in their opinion — is the connection between an electric light and a television set on the one hand, and the ability to explain the essence and purpose of things, to understand the creation of the world, to find the meaning of life and to define a code of behavior for human inter-relationships on the other hand.

The replies are almost always unsubstantiated claims that man has changed, man has become more perfect, more refined. Life itself is different now, they say. The structure, ideals and driving forces of society have changed, they say, as well as the motives of individual actions and the set of values which controls them.

And then I must show my audience the absurdity of its claims. No scientific progress or technology is capable of spiritually or morally perfecting a human being, of changing the essence or meaning of life, of influencing the factors which measure human happiness and satisfaction, of changing human passion, feeling, or motivations. In moral-ethical spheres, the life of man and society has not changed, not in hundreds of years nor in thousands of years.

It is enough to randomly open any book of the Bible, to leaf through any tractate of the Mishna, in order to become convinced that two or three thousand years ago, just like today, people lived and died, raised children, loved and hated, rejoiced and suffered, envied and sympathized with one another. Man's fate was just as full of vicissitudes and chance and just as inscrutable. Just as now, there were then greedy people and generous people, egoists and altruists, those who valued friendship and confidence and those who suffered from treachery and suspicion. In theory they upheld righteousness, honesty and uprightness, but in deed, they lied, cheated and dissembled. There were the same temptations then as today. Just as now, the ambition and lust for gain harbored by a few individuals in ages past could throw an entire people into torment. Not in vain did King Solomon say that "There is nothing new under the sun." Man has not become more noble by switching from riding a donkey or a horse to driving a luxury automobile. Man's soul, his aspirations, his capacity for happiness have not been improved by replacing candles with electric lights and definitely not by replacing books with movies. On the contrary, all these technological innovations, as everyone knows now, destroy nature and maim the soul.

Concerning refinement and spiritual perfection, it is enough merely to recall that in the Pale of Settlement there was not a single Jew who did not know how to answer questions about the essence of the soul and the essence of matter, about the purpose of man, about the origin of the world — whereas today university professors contrive to exist without any world outlook at all to embrace these issues. And even the claim that modern man is more competent professionally is also a myth. For the ancient specialist in steel, it was enough to look at a sword or to touch it with his hand to detect defects in manufacture, whereas today's metallurgists, armed to the teeth with spectroscopy and ultrasonic fault detection devices, sometimes struggle for years to remove the reason of a defect. Modern doctors, with all their electronic and other special equipment, with their thousands of sophisticated tests, hardly remember that the object of their work is a human being. And in the end sometimes it turns out that they can do less than a doctor aided only by his own thought and intuition a hundred years ago.

The best illustration of the fact that scientific progress improves neither man nor mankind is space travel, particularly the flights to the moon. Thirty years ago, when we were children, we would devour science-fiction novels describing man's adventures in space. We were convinced, along with the authors, that this grandiose achievement was going to change everybody and everything on the face of the earth. This happy future simply took our breath away. And now man has visited the moon, more than once; but not only have injustice, blood-shed, and hunger not decreased, but the man on the streets has long since forgotten that there ever were lunar flights.

Thus, since scientific-technological progress bears no influence on that which is truly important to us — on our character, on our capacity to love and hate, on our consciousness, on our feeling of duty, or even on our understanding of ourselves and the world we live in — then why is it commonly thought that science negates faith?

Our generation imagines that its adopted atheism and nihilism are the natural world outlooks both for mankind in general and for Jews in particular. The souls of our secular youngsters are not conscious of the generation of the desert led by Moshe Rabbeinu to become a People through receiving the Torah. They have no conception of how hundreds of generations of Jews suffered in order to keep their faith pure and whole. They have no idea how the recent generations have been gradually losing their faith, how the German and French Emancipation, the Jewish "enlightenment" movement, the eminent German Bible critic Wellhausen, and the dazzling growth of the natural sciences tempted so many of our grandfathers to deviate from the upright path of Judaism.

My audiences further give me old, hackneyed arguments that the findings of science negate the Torah. So of course I tell them, explaining in great detail, that it is nonsense to assume that science, which deals with the mutual inter-relationships of phenomena in the material world, can be contrasted or compared with the Torah, which interprets the spiritual sphere of life, the sphere of morality and ethics, and provides comprehensive, all-embracing answers to questions about Creation and about the essence, interconnection and purpose of all things in the universe and the universe itself.

Innumerable times I have had to answer questions about the six days of Creation. So many people dreadfully want to understand these days as periods of millions of years. If only they could realize that the very creation of the world by God *ex nihilo* is by far a greater miracle than the fact that it was completed in six days!

Once I tried to explain to my audience the essence of the concept of a *tzaddik*. I said that living strictly according to the Torah, subordinating personal and physical needs, constantly studying Torah and penetrating into its deepest secrets, and uplifting himself through prayer elevate such a Jew and qualify him to mediate between God and Israel. Thus, a *tzaddik* can reveal otherwise unseen things to his fellow Jews. The people in the audience, who considered themselves to be terribly intelligent and modern, were greatly annoyed by all this. One man even came up to me after the lecture to express his surprise that I—a man of science, a natural scientist (that's how he characterized me)—should be trying to fool a sophisticated audience with naïve fairy tales.

The next time that I had occasion to lecture on a similar theme to a similar audience, I decided to carry out a psychological experiment. Again I spoke about the supernatural gifts of the *tzaddik*, but this time I masked my talk in scientific imagery. I not only used terminology like "parapsychology" and "telepathy," but I also expanded on "thought-energy fields," about spaces with more than three dimensions and, after writing a lengthy differential equation on the blackboard, I chattered about quantum mechanics. Everything that I said was sheer nonsense — scientific-sounding verbiage. But you should have seen the hypnotic effect it had upon the audience and how many questions they respectfully asked me. Curiously enough, no one in the audience stood up to inform me that I was speaking nonsense from the purely scientific point of view. And that was an audience composed entirely of university graduates!

It turns out that such people base their belief neither on the strength of ideological reasons, nor on the results of logical analysis, nor on the basis of a well thought-out investigation. They simply have gotten into the habit of rejecting everything that sounds like religion and automatically accepting everything that sounds like science.

It is curious and sad that, tormented by the pace and strain of modern life, there are people, lonely within their swarming human ant colonies and hounded by fears, who are easily taken in by merchants of every possible cheap merchandise like yoga, Indian transcendental meditation and other forms of paganism and witchcraft. To join any of these modern cults of idolatry no intellectual deposit or effort is required, no self-restraint is needed. Everything is easy and accessible. Moreover, they spice their wares with pseudo-scientific references to physics, biology, psychology. This hypnotizes people into swallowing the bait, while it never occurs to them that their grandfathers, who rose before sunrise to study their daily lesson of Torah, put on *tefillin* and pray, and then worked sixteen hours a day while raising ten children, didn't need either yoga or meditation and didn't worry about "stresses," even though their physical life was a series of pogroms, hunger and other dangers.

56 I explain to my audiences why they must return to Torah and to the *mitzvoth*. I explain to them that they are depriving themselves by remaining passive outsiders to the eternal values of Judaism.

This essential return can be carried out on at least three levels. The first level is purely personal and individual. A man of faith has strict order in his life. He has clear aims. He knows where to find the answers to disturbing questions. Having an integral world outlook, he therefore has a greater chance to achieve inner harmony and peace. He has upon Whom to rely and from whence to derive confidence for the future. To the extent that he succeeds in bringing up his children in this spirit, they will respect and honor him and be protected from vices raging in the modern world, such as drugs, perversion and violence.

Religion, faith and a sense of the constant presence of God overseeing every human step are the most secure means of self-defense that a young person can have. To use one of Notke's analogies: just as a car without brakes can't be driven, so a human being without a protective system of self-control inevitably becomes sacrificed to his own inherent source of evil, pulling him to lusts and passions.

And here is one final important point concerning personal happiness. No matter how hard a Jew tries to assimilate, no matter how much he disguises himself in alien attire, he is not free from belonging to Judaism (unless, of course, he crosses over the final border of physical assimilation — of inter-marrying and raising his children as non-Jews — against which many non-identifying Jews still retain an inner aversion). Sooner or later the moment comes when the enemy reminds him that he is a Jew. This is an empirical fact. And then, when this inevitably does happen, lacking the treasures of the Jewish soul, seeing no reason to be proud of belonging to the Jewish people and ignorant of its purpose in the world, he takes his Jewishness as an everlasting, inescapable curse. And then the life of this Jew running away from his own self becomes a real hell. It never occurs to him that his very own parents robbed him, deprived him of an ideal and a guiding thread in life. Out of a mistaken notion of love for their children, the parents of such a lost Jew struggled to integrate their sons and daughters into a "culture common to all mankind," to give them an "intellectual profession," and to take them out of the "world of the *shtetl*" into the "big world."

The Almighty said to the Jews in the Torah: "Here I give you a blessing and a curse, life and death. Choose life." Every Jew has to make this choice, and the tragedy is compounded when a person's children and grandchildren are deprived because of his mistaken decision.

The second of the three necessary levels of return is national. We became a nation in an entirely different way from all other nations. Usually groups of people become a nation as a result of having lived together for a long time, occupying the same territory, and having built an economy and a system of social attitudes. But we became a nation on the fiftieth day after the exodus from Egypt when, standing at the foot of Mount Sinai, we accepted the yoke of the Torah, saying: "*Na'aseh venishma*." Torah and faith united us from the very onset. Everything else was secondary and resulting from this source. Ironically, our enemies consider us a most calculating people. But the truth is that we were born as a nation in an irrational way, and all our subsequent history has also been completely irrational. Our most noteworthy deeds demonstrate that in critical moments, free of all calculations and logic, we stand ready to sacrifice ourselves. Thus, it is not surprising that the Marxists do not recognize us as a nation. In their own way, they are being consistent. People who have forced human consciousness to fit into a narrow, rigid, cramped, primitive, Procrustean bed are not able to accept the

Jewish people or even to recognize its existence. It is simply beyond their comprehension.

Since the Jewish people arose thanks to and for the sake of the Torah, naturally it can exist only in connection with the Torah. For those who accept and realize this simple truth, further explanation is unnecessary. However, insofar as most of us have been educated in scepticism and rationalism, I must also present here rational explanations based on history and national experience.

It is a fact that the Jewish people has lost more of its sons to assimilation during the entire course of its history than to the monstrous periods of destruction of ancient Rome, the Inquisition, the pogroms, Bogdan Chmielnicki and Hitler. Those who assimilated were those who abandoned the Torah. Statistics show that families who abandon the Torah, the *mitzvoth* and tradition can manage to avoid physical assimilation at the most for four generations or, in rare cases, five generations. (This pertains to Israel just as much as to the countries of the Diaspora.) Even the most extreme atheists agree that religion is the main and even sole factor which preserved our people for thousands of years. However, they are convinced that now things have changed and this factor can be thrown away. In addition to their old argument that our modern age is a special one, they refer to the fact of the existence of the State of Israel. They forget that:

a) the danger of assimilation is possibly even greater for those Jews breaking away from tradition within Israel itself than for those in other countries where the hostility of the environment impedes assimilation somewhat;

b) there is no more convincing proof of our right to our land than the fact that it was commanded by God to Abraham, Isaac and Jacob for eternity (a fact well known by any Christian or Moslem);

c) were it not for the Torah and the *mitzvoth*, even if we had physically survived until today, we simply would not know that we once had a land in the Middle East. And even if we did know about it from history and archeology, without the practice of our religion we wouldn't think that this land still bears any relation to us today.

If more empirical proof is needed to show the importance and inevitability of returning to the Torah after the establishment of the State, then consider the words of the Torah that we are "a people who dwells alone." Never has history so convincingly confirmed this than just after the proclamation of the State of Israel.

Here is one last analogy to conclude our discussion of the national level of return to Judaism. Most people nowadays have life insurance. This doesn't mean that they're getting ready to die. On the contrary, everyone hopes for a long and happy life. Well then, isn't it time to start thinking about life insurance on a national level? We all believe and hope that our new state will last forever. However, as serious people, it is incumbent upon us to consider the worst possibility. And if we do this, then we immediately discover that if the younger generation raised in Israel were forced, God forbid, to go into exile, their ability to resist assimilation would be a thousand times worse than was that of the previous generations of the Diaspora. Alas, children of non-traditional families would be simply defenseless against alien influences. It would probably take not even an entire generation, but only a number of years, to bring about their absolute assimilation.

And, finally, let us discuss the third level upon which it is necessary to return to the Torah — the philosophical level. As my book *From the Depths* deals with this subject, I shall not elaborate here. I shall simply recall its major conclusion. And that is that the Torah contains the only possible irrefutable explanation of the essence of the universe, its origin and existence, and also of the essence and purpose of the Jewish people. It also reveals the essence, origin and purpose of all things. The Torah contains truths which are tightly sealed and inaccessible to the rational mind, acquainted only with relationships and phenomena. These categories of the essence, origin and purpose of Creation are conveyed to man in the Torah, revealing to those who perceive it the highest knowledge which a mortal being can possess. Whether you accept and recognize this knowledge or not depends on you. But even if you reject it, it doesn't cease being the truth.

A Jew can believe or not believe, accept the Torah or not accept it — this is actually the only degree of liberty that he has. Whatever choice the Jew makes, it will determine his fate, although nobody imposes a decision upon him. For everything else except this free choice, however, there operates a universal and inviolable predestination — the direct manifestation of the will of the all-penetrating presence of God.

Whether someone likes this truth or doesn't like it bears no influence upon the truth itself. A "revolt" against the truth of the Torah has even less significance than someone "revolting" against the laws of gravity by jumping out the window or protesting against the necessity of breathing by putting his head in a plastic bag.

And here I often have the opportunity to add one more argument to my case. The Torah cannot be penetrated by cold reasoning and analysis. It is impossible to feel the happiness and joy of a Torah life by looking in from the outside. Torah must be tasted. Torah cannot be understood only by the intellect. The heart, soul and intuition must be involved. The world of Torah must be entered and lived through, not just for a day or two, but until the scab of many years peels off the soul, revealing secret sensitive receptors, and a long slumbering forgotten "I" rejoices, "Yes, this is my very own Jewish self — this is what I was meant to be."

57 It yet remains for me to express my boundless gratitude to the Almighty for giving me the chance to return — to make my *teshuva* — and for providing me with guidance. In my recollections I review the thirty years since I started to search for the blessing in being Jewish, stressing the last fifteen years since I put on my *tefillin* for the first time and thus became a Jew by deeds and not just by conviction. What would my life have been without the return? But that is an idle question. Instead of dealing with it I have tried to explain to myself and to others what I have found thanks to the *teshuva*.

But, although I have tried to give the answer on the philosophical level, on the national level and on quite a number of other levels, one simple human aspect remains that I have probably still not put into words clearly enough on the preceding pages. And that is how good it is to be a Jew openly and proudly and to know clearly what it means to be a Jew. All the words in the world would not suffice to explain the joy of going to the synagogue in Russia, or to a Torah class, or to a Chassidic gathering. To move through the hostile mob, to sense the eyes of the shadowers on your back and to remain proud and confident. How sorry I am for those still there who did not yet return and who still are — as I was years ago — continually ready to melt into their surroundings, to annihilate self, to imitate, to feign . . .

But is it really just there, in Russia? Did I not meet hundreds and hundreds of American Jews who are doing exactly the same? Moreover, did I not see even observant American Jews, even members of an association of Orthodox scientists, who shame-facedly hide their *yarmulkes* in their pockets as soon as they reach the threshold of their university or laboratory? Yes, years ago I did the same. But now, thank God, I learned that the gentile colleague respects you more when you explain to him that you cannot have a "normal" dinner at his home. And there have been many cases when gentile professors, even without my reminder, prepared special kosher meals (ordered from the suppliers to airline companies) for me at scientific conferences, or invited me home for a meal of fresh, unpeeled fruit, served specially on new plastic dishes, or finally when a gentile colleague at a meeting Friday afternoon looked at his watch with worry and said, "You have to rush — it's almost your Sabbath."

These may seem to be mere trifles, but they make you feel at peace with yourself. And even more important, they make you be whom you are truly meant to be.

And finally I wish to add one more expression of my unending gratitude to the Almighty Who, in this world filled with lies and illusions, has let me taste the truth and delight in some small measure in knowing Him and His *mitzvoth*. I am infinitely fortunate that, after having gone through many errors, now I can repeat the principles of faith of the great Rambam with a clear conscience and complete belief:

1. I believe with perfect faith that the Creator, blessed be His Name, creates and guides all the created beings, and that He alone has made, does make, and will make all things.
2. I believe with perfect faith that the Creator, blessed be His Name, is a unity, and that there is no oneness of any kind like His, and that He alone is our God, Who was, is, and will be.
3. I believe with perfect faith that the Creator, blessed be His Name, is not corporeal, and that He is free from all the properties of matter, and that He has not any likeness whatsoever.
4. I believe with perfect faith that the Creator, blessed be His Name, was the first and will be the last.
5. I believe with perfect faith that the Creator, blessed be His Name, is the only one to whom it is proper to pray, and that it is not proper to pray to any being besides Him.

6. I believe with perfect faith that all the words of the prophets are true.

7. I believe with perfect faith that the prophecy of Moshe Rabbeinu, peace be unto him, was true, and that he was the chief of the prophets, both to those who preceded and to those who followed.

8. I believe with perfect faith that the whole Torah now in our possession is the same that was given to Moshe Rabbeinu, peace be unto him.

9. I believe with perfect faith that this Torah will not be changed, and that there will be no other Torah from the Creator, blessed be His Name.

10. I believe with perfect faith that the Creator, blessed be His Name, knows every deed of human beings and all their thoughts, as it is said: "Who fashions the hearts of them all, Who comprehends all their deeds."

11. I believe with perfect faith that the Creator, blessed be His Name, rewards those who keep His commandments and punishes those who transgress His commandments.

12. I believe with perfect faith in the coming of the Messiah; and although he may tarry, I will wait daily for his coming.

13. I believe with perfect faith that there will be a revival of the dead at the time when it shall please the Creator, blessed be His Name, and exalted be His mention forever and ever.

Beersheva,
5737 years after the Creation
(1976 in the non-Jewish calendar)